The Art of

Hello®

BE REMEMBERED
IN A NOISY WORLD™

PAULA CALISE

Dedication

WILL REED
GONE BUT NEVER
FORGOTTEN

This book and every word I speak and teach on The Art of Hello® are dedicated to the memory of William C. Reed II, my precious son.

To William – beloved son, brother, nephew, cousin, friend. The kindest person we have ever known. You are missed and will be always in our hearts.

Acknowledgments

In the tradition of *it takes a village*, this book, *The Art of Hello®* was written. First, for always giving me a wide berth to be and do my own thing, while loving and supporting me, I thank Bill Reed, my dear husband. I thank my accomplished daughter Andrea Reed, who encouraged me and appreciated my work almost as much as I appreciate hers. Andrea was the final copy editor of the book and is the artist of the block print at the end of each chapter. Thank you to my marketing genius friends, Rita Egeland and Tracey Altman. They lent their discerning eyes to the cover and the interior book design. Thank you, Jason Tinelle, my multi-talented nephew, for selecting the cover font for *The Art of Hello®* – such a perfect choice for this book. Thank you, Randy Mayeux, business book reader extraordinaire, and monthly First Friday Book Synopsis event leader. Randy's guidance on the story that a Table of Contents tells helped me hone the whole story of the book. Thank you, Toni Point, the block print artist who with the patience of a saint created the prints that open every chapter and close the book.

Thank you to Michelle Prince and the editorial and artistic team at Performance Publishing Group. And lastly, but perhaps most importantly, I thank the many thousands of people who have attended The Art of Hello® presentations. I have received hundreds of positive reviews and comments about the impact that an Art of Hello® introduction can make for professionals at every point in their careers. It was through those comments that I knew I was onto something fresh and something that needed to be shared.

The Art of Hello® helps professionals deliver a brand introduction that's memorable and impactful. In her book, Paula Calise gives you a practical framework and enlightening stories to guide you in creating your perfect brand. As an award-winning recruiter, she's an expert on this topic.

Shaunna Black,
President of Shaunna Black and Associates

Table of Contents

Introduction

The "So What" Conundrum

It was a really hot day filled with appointments. My lunch meeting at La Madeleine was with a woman named Karen,[1*] whom I had never met before. I scanned the restaurant and saw someone fitting her description sitting near the window; I headed that way. After introducing myself, I immediately asked, "Karen, could you help me out, please?" I said, "I am not very well prepared for our discussion. I printed out your resume but left it on my desk, and I haven't looked at your LinkedIn profile. I'd really appreciate it if you'd tell me about yourself."

Without hesitation, Karen began detailing her career to that point. She was, at the time, the vice president of marketing for Mary Kay Cosmetics. "I have been with the company for 18 years," she said, "all of it in the

---

1 * All of the stories told here are true. Some names and minor details have been changed for the sake of privacy.

marketing department. Anything to do with marketing, I've done it."

Then she offered a list of the specific areas of her expertise, "I've done collateral; I've put on large events and directed successful promotions." She continued, "I've supervised both qualitative and quantitative research."

Her recitation included working in social media, public relations, and crisis communications. And, she said, "I've liaised with product developers on color theory and with designers on packaging and labeling…"

As Karen droned on and on and on, I was thinking **"So what? So what? So what?"**

It's hard to imagine that anyone in this day and age could rise to the position of vice president of marketing in a significant global company without having all of the experience Karen listed—and more. Those skills are table stakes—the minimum entry requirements—in her field. Though I'm sure it was not her intention, what Karen was telling me was "I'm ordinary."

No one wants to be thought of as ordinary. But for people to get to know the *extra*ordinary person you are, they must first *remember* who you are. That's where The Art of Hello comes in. This distinctive technique cuts the old elevator speech down to a statement so concise that new acquaintances will be able to repeat it after hearing it only once, and people who know you well can pass it on, perfectly.

Throughout this book, you'll meet people whose stories illustrate the power of The Art of Hello. You'll also learn the three simple steps that will help you create your very own Art of Hello introduction.

The Art of Hello® = What every professional needs to know about building a personal brand introduction.

Chapter One
Success Starts with Being Remembered

We'll return to Karen later, but first, let me introduce myself. My name is Paula Calise. I'm an executive recruiter, and *I fill hard to fill positions*. In business, that is the most important thing for people to know about me. I'm an executive recruiter, and *I fill hard to fill positions*.

I've been using that succinct brand label for myself since I started my recruiting firm over a decade ago.

> I have a simple-to-remember Art of Hello introduction: *I'm Paula Calise—I fill hard to fill positions.*

Having a memorable label, and living up to what it promises, has paid off. Today, 100 percent of my business is repeat clients or referrals from my friends and colleagues, as well as from past and current clients. I consider these people my large, latent salesforce. This network can refer clients to me because they know, absolutely, what I do. They can recite my brand exactly and pass it on easily because I have a simple-to-remember Art of Hello introduction: *I'm Paula Calise—I fill hard to fill positions.*

That's it. Those six simple words tell people everything they need to know about me. Occasionally, when appropriate, I will follow up by explaining that I fill jobs that have gone unfilled for six weeks or six months. I am often called in when a job can't be filled by someone else. This is how I have introduced myself from the start, and it's what I say to the new people I meet every day. When I go to meetings, colleagues walk up to me and say, "Hey, Paula, I want you to meet Randy. Randy, this is my friend Paula. She's an executive recruiter. *She fills hard to fill positions.*"

Boom.

I get introduced by others exactly the way I introduce myself. It's my brand. There's no ambiguity about it. It's absolutely clear, simple, and truthful. Because people can remember and repeat who I am and what I do, my colleagues, friends, and acquaintances have become my brand advocates.

Building a Brand Advocate Base

Brand advocates are the primary reason I have come to be a bit of a zealot about personal brand introductions. The business-building results I get from a clean and consistent self-introduction pay off in referral and recruiting fees. I know my "salesforce" is out there spreading the word when I get calls from hiring managers and internal company recruiters saying they heard that *I fill hard to fill positions*, asking if I can help them fill one. My answer is always, "Why, yes. I can."

My brand advocates are not just nice to have—they are a *must* have—and they often come to me in unusual ways. In Chapter Three, I will share an example of a referral that came to me in quite an extraordinary way and is 100 percent attributed to my easy-to-remember self-introduction.

> Brand advocates are a must have.

Being Remembered or Not Being Remembered Are Your Only Choices

The second reason I am an introduction zealot is because I've learned the hard way that people, myself included, are forgetful. I have been an executive recruiter for about a decade and a half. In that time, I've met and spoken to thousands of people, not only the people I have interviewed, which is a lot, but also the people I've met over the course of my 35-year career conducting business and serving the community. Serving on boards and attending meetings of various kinds means I meet people every-where I go. That should be good for business, right? The problem is, of the thousands of people I have met over the years, there are very few I remember—maybe 10 per-cent. And keep in mind, I'm a connector! Professionally and personally, I connect people. I connect people to jobs or to other people nearly every single day.

If I forget most of the people I meet, whose loss is it? If I can't remember someone, I can't connect them to jobs or to other opportunities. That makes it my loss as well as theirs. People I meet might gain something if I could remember who they are and what they do. I know I would gain by remembering them. But I don't.

People remembering my name and brand while I for-get theirs is a stark reminder of the power of a memora-ble personal brand introduction. You would rather be in the remembered camp than the forgotten one. This book is filled with what I've learned about creating a mem-orable introduction. My aspiration is for you to have a memorable introduction that will serve you, as mine has served me.

When I realized that I wanted to speak on the subject of helping people create memorable, simple-to-under-stand, and impactful introductions, I did what anyone would do: I went to Google and started researching. The results affirmed my assumption that the help provided online is outdated, at best.

The Dubious Elevator Speech and 30-Second Drill

There are at least two philosophies on personal introductions. The first and oldest is the "elevator speech." The earliest reference to this short form of introduction comes from Philip Crosby, author of *The Art of Getting Your Own Sweet Way*. Crosby suggested that individuals should have a prepared speech about themselves that they can deliver in the time it takes to ride an elevator.[2] The idea is that if you happen to be in that enclosed space with an executive you want to impress, you'll have about 30 seconds to make your impression before the trapped executive can escape.

A lot has been written since Crosby first proffered this technique. Today, hundreds of articles, books, posts, and YouTube lessons expound the various ways of mastering the art of introduction. There are even tournaments in which contestants compete to best each other in making introductions. Some of the suggested approaches are more complicated than others, such as *17 Steps to the Best Elevator Speech*. YIKES! Mastering 17 steps sounds so complicated. With 17 steps involved, how is the resulting introduction supposed to be clear and memorable?

The concept of the elevator speech emerged before the Internet Age. Now, a tsunami of information floods our brains from a zillion social media outlets, all available at our fingertips. It's easy to understand how, as

---

2 Philip Crosby, *The Art of Getting Your Own Sweet Way*, Mcgraw-Hill, 1972.

researchers tell us, the amount of information available to us doubles every 12 hours.[3]

A face-to-face introduction is just one data point in the sea of information that a person receives daily. As people are inundated with constant content, they learn to tune it out, and that is one of the drawbacks of elevator speeches—people have become pros at tuning them out.

Additionally, in recent years, an elevator speech has come to mean little more than knowing what to say about yourself and what you are looking for when you are in a job search. I take issue with this narrow application of the effective introduction.

In most of the elevator-speech literature, a person is expected to include a few words about their goal or objective and what they want out of the introduction. It likely comes across as:

- I'm looking for an opportunity to…

   or

- I'm looking for my next big challenge…

Why would a person say that? The best way to make the person you meet turn on their heels and run is to start a conversation by telling them what you want from them. It is simply too self-centered. As you read further about The Art of Hello, you'll learn how to turn the

3   Gary Woodill, "Rapid Doubling of Knowledge Drives Change in How We Learn," *Float*, January 23, 2018, Retrieved on December 22, 2020 from https://gowithfloat.com/2018/01/rapid-doubling-knowledge-drives-change-learn/.

introduction paradigm on its head and *focus on what you can deliver, not on what you can get.*

> Turn the introduction paradigm on its head and *focus on what you can deliver, not on what you can get.*

I agree with the old, elevator-speech thinking that, during a job search, it's good to be prepared and to know what you will say about yourself if you're given the opportunity. My problem with it, however, is that well-prepared introductions leave out a large group of people—business owners, company and organization executives and employees, and professionals of all varieties—who are not looking for a job. What about that segment of professionals? Little is written and less is shared about all of us who understand the value of making effective introductions. Keep reading, and we will get there together.

A slight update to the elevator pitch is the 30-second drill or (God forbid) the 90-second drill. Memorizing uselessly long and boring monologues about oneself is a good way to become easily and immediately forgotten. These speeches tend to include pointless declarations of the job seeker's "great leadership

> 30-second drill is *not memorable* because of the level of detail.

ability, attention to detail, and trustworthiness." They also assert that they are "hard-working, a great listener, creative, a team player, solution driven, seasoned, a strategic visionary who is highly motivated, and has superior interpersonal skills that foster positive cultures." Oh, and you always get a few "out-of-the-box thinkers."

So, I ask you, who isn't a leader, listener, team player, and motivated to succeed? Or who will admit it if they are not? Okay, maybe not all of us will sink to the "out-of-the-box thinker" nonsense, but we've all heard the rest of the qualities on that list.

The Elevator Speech —and Its Tired Friend the 30-Second Drill—Are Dead... Long Live The Art of Hello®!

As professionals, we all deserve to be known for our achievements and to be understood for our value proposition. Using the old-fashioned elevator speech or 30-second drill works against us as professionals.

- Knowledge doubles every 12 hours; information is flooding us. One of the drawbacks of boring elevator speeches is that people have become pros at tuning them out.

- The elevator speech and 30-second drill are simply too self-centered, people are more interested in themselves than in you.

- Memorized and uselessly long, boring monologues about oneself are easily and immediately forgotten.

- The elevator speech and 30-second drill are not memorable because of the level of detail.

- Using an elevator speech can make you look like someone who can't net-it-out. It does not demonstrate executive presence.

- Elevator speeches are packed with pointless self-declarations.

- Elevator speeches and 30-second drills are not the way to be known and remembered when trying to get a job.

What's wrong with the 30-second drill? First, it's *too long*. I heard this pitch recently, offered by a diligent executive who clearly put a lot of time in crafting, memorizing, and delivering her elevator speech. It is like a Wikipedia entry of her life and career stuffed into about 30 seconds. Here it is:

I am a senior manager in commercial insurance with a focus in multi-state workers' comp claim programs and risk consulting. I drive profitability and compliance via accountability, responsibility, and flexibility. I thrive in creating environments that are diverse, inclusive, and even a little fun. I am a dynamic, principled, inclusive leader who builds teams and creates cultures of success, where individual skills are developed, providing an exceptional customer experience, and I meet or exceed company goals. I accomplish company goals, personal development, and meet or exceed customer expectations.

That is 88 words.

The second problem with the 30-second drill is that it is *not memorable* because of the level of detail. When this gal finished, I couldn't remember her name or profession because I was so focused on the details and so distracted by her practiced-to-perfection recitation.

Finally, if you believe in the adage that first impressions count, then don't be known as someone who can't net-it-out, who can't give an executive summary of oneself. Here is my Art of Hello recommendation for this executive:

> *Through workers comp insurance, I return injured workers to work sooner.*

That is 11 words.

Which would you find more memorable?

A note here about first impressions. Whether it's done right or wrong, your self-introduction is, by its very nature, the first impression you make. We have all heard that you never get a second chance to make a good first impression—your first impression may also be your last impression. No matter the adage, the fact is that when you first meet people, they make a judgment about you in approximately seven seconds. According to some sources, people form their whole impression of you within 27 seconds of initial contact.[4]

In the 88-word example above, by the time the 30-second drill has been regurgitated, the clock has run out, and you will get nothing else; the sticky first impression is set. People actively listen for only 30 seconds on a good day, and they are more intent on their self-interest than they are on yours. Yes, it is true, even in cases where you think

> Retire your elevator speech and its friend the 30-second drill. There is a better way.

it would be otherwise. For example, consider a job interview in which a person has every reason to be focused on you; after all, they invited you in, presumably. Right

---

4   Peter Economy, "According to This Truly Surprising New Study, You Have Just 27 Seconds to Make a First Impression," *Inc.* December 29, 2018, Retrieved on December 22, 2020 from https://www.inc.com/peter-economy/according-to-this-truly-surprising-new-study-you-have-just-27-seconds-to-make-a-first-impression.html.

off the bat, the interviewer is sizing you up. As you get started telling them a bit about yourself, the interviewer is already thinking, *Will this person lighten my load? Will I look good making this hire? Will they stay with the company? Will they try to take my job and push me out?* If your introduction is self-focused and doesn't convey your brand promise simply, clearly, and quickly—thus, catching the interviewer's attention—you are sunk.

The Art of Hello is a fresh approach to being remembered. For those who find themselves in a job search, crafting an Art of Hello-branded introduction is a must. For the rest of us, it's a career asset we cannot afford to be without.

Come on the journey with me.

The Art of Hello® at a Glance

Chapter One

- Talking too much can trigger the "SO WHAT" response

- The elevator speech and the 30-second drill make you forgettable

- The Art of Hello will teach you a better way — I promise

Chapter Two

Distilling Your Professional Life

The Art of Hello distills[5*] your professional life to its core. It is not a list of everything you've ever done in your career. It is not a litany of every single credential you've ever earned, every skill you've learned, every job you've had, or every accomplishment you are proud of. It is not a thesaurus of terms in your industry. It is not a list of your previous positions. The Art of Hello is a distillation of your professional life. It takes the most important parts and puts them into a few words that tell others how you want to be known and *remembered*. The Art of Hello introduction nets out who you are, and

---

5   * distill (dis·till | \ di-ˈstil) transitive verb meaning to extract the essence.

more importantly, it expresses the promise you make to those who engage with you professionally. It is your professional brand. (This could be the most important paragraph of this book. You might want to read it again.)

As you learned in the previous chapter, I am not a fan of the 30-second drill or the elevator speech. They are too long, are not memorable, and do not demonstrate an executive presence. Out with the old, in with The Art of Hello.

The second reason why I forget so many of the people I meet has to do with personal branding. The "personal brand" nomenclature is credited to Tom Peters in a 1997 Fast Company article.[6] Today, personal branding is everywhere—it is the subject of entire books, hundreds of blog posts, and hour upon hour of YouTube content. Much of personal branding in popular culture is aimed at making the reader, listener, or watcher into a Kardashian, metaphorically speaking. These branding authorities focus on making their adherents into well-known, well-followed experts on something—anything.

> The Art of Hello is a distillation of your professional life. It takes the most important parts and puts them into a few words that tell others how you want to be known and *remembered*.

---

6   Tom Peters, "The Brand Called You", *Fast Company*, August 8, 1997, Retrieved on December 22, 2020 from https://www.fastcompany.com/28905/brand-called-you.

The following pages are filled with a very different approach to personal branding. I have not yet met anyone who seeks personal brand *fame*. My daily experiences tell me that most of us just want to master our professions, grow our businesses, and lead generally fruitful lives away from the glare of followers.

As professionals, we all deserve to be known for our achievements and to be understood for our value proposition. The core of personal branding is to introduce yourself in a way that the listener understands the essence of your professional life. Once scripted and perfected, your branded introduction is a durable asset. It will serve as your networking introduction, your LinkedIn profile summary, the opening to your bio, and as the professional summary of your resume. It will even function as a succinct introduction during internal meetings with new partners or executives, both in person and online.

Crafting your own succinct professional brand statement helps people remember you. That is what you deserve for the hard work, long hours, education, certifications, pain-in-the-neck bosses, and the all-around effort you've put into your career. With a clear and concise statement, you can make the most of each opportunity.

How Clarity Can Help Build Your Business

A well-conceived personal branded introduction takes the idea behind the old-fashioned elevator pitch and polishes it up to a professional sheen with memorable impact. It differentiates you from others. It is so simple to recognize when done well, but so hard to make one your own.

It is not by accident that my introduction is clear; it is by design. (I am an executive recruiter, and *I fill hard to fill positions*—have you forgotten?) The journey through this book will provide you with the career-building tools that have benefitted my career. What's more, these tools are free, and having them offers an enormous ROI for the small amount of time it takes to craft an Art of Hello introduction. Crafting a memorable introduction may be one of the best investments you ever make in your career.

So, how do you introduce yourself? Is your brand introduction impactful to the person you're meeting? Does it differentiate you from other people who might have similar backgrounds or professions? Is it authentic? Does your introduction suit you? Does it represent you well and honestly? And, most of all, will it be remembered?

Apply the principles clearly outlined here and you will come away with something that you may have never thought about before. When you introduce yourself to the world in this new way, you'll have a great payoff, no matter the setting.

> Crafting a memorable introduction may be one of the best investments you ever make in your career.

I will define an easy-to-use, three-step process showing how you can assume a brand position you can claim as your own and by which people will come to know you. It will be a statement that is unique and that differentiates you from others in your profession. This exercise will help you create a memorable and impactful branded introduction, useful to anyone who cares about their career. It is useful for emerging professionals, for senior leaders, for those seeking positions on boards, and for job seekers. It is effective for anyone who has a business to build, a career to nurture, something to sell, and for those who just want to live among us without being a hermit.

Come and join me.

A Lightbulb Moment

First, let's reconnect with Karen, our Mary Kay marketing executive, who forced me into the "So what?" mode.

Since I had not actually said "So what?" out loud, Karen continued listing the tactical work of her marketing career. Finally, I had to stop her. "Karen," I said, "hold on a minute. Let me redirect the conversation a little bit. I am not a Mary Kay cosmetics user," I explained, "but being here in Dallas where Mary Kay is headquartered, I have noticed that Mary Kay looks a little different than it has in the past."

"Paula, thanks for noticing. About 16 months ago I embarked upon a brand refresh. We did not hire a branding or marketing company. Two colleagues and I trained ourselves regarding what our brand was and how to impact it. I have worked on, touched, or authored everything in our new brand."

Okay, now we have something interesting. Here's Karen working on her company's brand. And not only does she modernize it because she had pre- and post-testing proof, but she also did much of the work herself. Karen moved the needle, and her fingerprints are all over the results. So, I thought for a minute and said to her, "Karen, if I'm hearing you correctly, *you are an expert at revitalizing tired brands.*"

Karen had a light bulb moment. She said, "Yes, Paula, as a matter of fact, I am. I'm now an expert at revitalizing tired brands."

So, dear reader, I ask you—which of the following introductions sounds more memorable?

> Hi, I'm Karen. I'm a vice president of marketing, and I do programs and I do collateral. I do market research. I work online and offline. I work in public relations and community relations. I work crisis communications and plan meetings and conferences, and I work on color theory, blah, blah, blah.

Or,

> Hi, I'm Karen. I'm a marketing executive, and I revitalize tired brands.

Boom. *That* is The Art of Hello.

What Is at Stake in a Misguided Introduction?

In highlighting what's expected of anyone in her position, Karen was making herself sound ordinary. By rattling off a list of everyday tactics that any professional in a job like hers has mastered, Karen wasn't telling me anything about herself that set her apart or made her memorable. She might as well have responded to my initial question to tell me about herself by saying "Oh, me? Nothing special here."

Karen was unable to tell me who she was at the core of her professional self. In the process, she lost me. She gave me a long list of marketing terms, like chapters from a college marketing primer. I could not recite or remember her whole list, so what was her intention? Was she trying to win me over via the tsunami method? Drown me in professional terms hoping to impress?

In truth, Karen was sincerely trying to describe her professional attributes. She wanted me to like her and help her. But her approach wasn't working, and it wasn't her fault. Karen hadn't

> Listing what's expected of anyone in your position is not the same as saying something about yourself and what makes you memorable.

been taught how to introduce herself. She had improved her professional skills over the years, as her litany of experience demonstrated, but she had not learned how to package her expertise into an introduction that others could appreciate when meeting her for the first time.

What I have left out of Karen's story is that when I met her in 2008, she, like millions of others, was about to fall victim to the Great Recession. She would be vice president of marketing for Mary Kay only one more week before she was laid off.

Unfortunately for Karen, she would be competing for a new job in a soft labor market. There was an abundance of unemployed marketing VPs that she would be competing against in the marketplace. Despite her 18 years of experience, her broad marketing practices, her apparent vivacity and willingness to work at job hunting, Karen was not ready for primetime. What was at stake on that hot day in Dallas was not just Karen's ability to get a job as good as the one she had lost but rather getting a job at all.

Here is the heart of the problem: had we not had the brand conversation, Karen was on her way to being forgotten when I walked out of the restaurant. Fortunately, after discovering a memorable self-introduction, Karen was able to attack her job search with an Art of Hello introduction: "I'm Karen, a VP of Marketing, and *I revitalize tired brands*." Now that's memorable.

The Art of Hello® at a Glance

Chapter Two

- The Art of Hello is the distillation of your professional life
- Be known for your achievements and your value proposition
- Clarity is king
- The stakes: being remembered or forgotten is in your hands

Chapter Three

Remembered or Forgotten?
That Is the Question

There is an archetype, or a category, for Karen's self-introduction. It is ***The Biggest, Baddest Thing I Have Done*** introduction. Because in Karen's career, *the biggest, baddest thing* she had ever done was revitalize a dated brand.

Nailing that down provided the essence of Karen's professional brand—her Art of Hello.

When we have an opportunity to introduce ourselves, there are only two possible results that can come from it. Either we are remembered, or we are forgotten.

There's not a lot of middle ground. Each of us has struggled to recall someone. "Oh, yes," you may say, "maybe I remember him; he's tall with dark hair? No?" Or, maybe, "I remember her. I think I met her at that conference, right?" What we are more honestly thinking is, *I have no idea who he/she is.* Blank, nada, nothing. Unfortunately, most of our first meetings with people fall into that category. Forgettable. Forgotten.

The tragedy is that the vast majority of the time, we are introducing ourselves with the sincere hope of being remembered. When we meet new people in business and social settings, we have usually placed ourselves there with the intention of networking.[7]* But rather than using the few moments we have with potential employers, clients, colleagues, and partners in a memorable way, we plow right into the realm of the forgotten. So, Karen is not alone—she has lots of company. In fact, she represents the majority of professionals struggling to describe themselves, babbling along, being forgotten even as they speak.

Recently, I talked with Kenton Kisler, executive director of Dallas' prestigious Executive Connections, about the topic of introductions. He told me that when a person is long winded while introducing themselves, he simply stops listening. Kenton told me that he tries to keep eye contact with the person and continues to nod, but he is really thinking, "What's for dinner tonight?"

---

7   * Networking is practiced by far too many people only when changing jobs. The power of a strong network should be used at all times.

Kenton's reaction is typical. We may be facing the person, smiling, with an occasional murmur or head nod, and yet we're not listening. Think of it this way, if you are more interested in whether or not you're having chicken tonight than you are in meeting the person right in front of you, there is no doubt that this introduction is already in the forgotten pile.

When we first met Karen, she was clearly on her way to being forgotten, not only by me but by anyone who might encounter her in her job search—including the hiring managers at her next potential employer. A vice president candidate will be interviewed by executives, so the hiring manager could be a company president or C-suite officer. It is not likely that these executives see value in a generic list of tasks.

Yet Karen, like many people, used the list method to introduce herself, and as a result, she missed a massive opportunity. And she is not alone. I meet people from every profession, every industry, every rung on the career ladder who use a list as a substitute for an impactful self-introduction. I hear a recitation of lists from engineers, software developers, accountants, administrative assistants, business consultants, HR executives, supply-chain experts, geologists, college students, scientists, captains of industry, and so many more. If you'd like to see some examples for yourself, go to LinkedIn and look at 20 or 30 random LinkedIn profiles. They are filled with lists of tactical work and industry acronyms and nomenclature.

As a recruiter who uses LinkedIn every day, I see this on an even larger scale. So many people look the same, and my "so what" meter clicks in. Many times, to find a great match for my clients' positions—using LinkedIn profiles as a starting point—I have to read between the lines and imagine what people are *not* saying that would be useful to me, the recruiter who is trying to make a match. Then, when I talk with people, I have to suss out the information I seek.

Resumes, too, are often simply lists of tactics, jargon, and acronyms. The one advantage with resumes, however, is that people have gotten the news that they need to quantify their achievements. Directionally better, but still, most resumes and LinkedIn profiles lack an easy to understand, definitive statement of who the person is at the essence of their professional life.

I had been hearing some good, but mostly poor, self-introductions for years. Then one day, I was moved to learn, and eventually, say more about the subject. It was in December of 2017, and I was in a small-group roundtable meeting with members of The University of Texas at Dallas Institute for Excellence in Corporate Governance (IECG). There were six members of the Institute, people like me, mature, senior profession-als—later in our careers, but not quite ready for the couch or the backyard garden—who were preparing to be candidates for private and public boards, or simply sharpening our skills in order to be more effective non-profit board members. The purpose of the roundtable was to get to know our fellow members so we would be better able to refer each other to board opportunities that we might discover.

As we made our way around the table, the first three introductions stopped me in my tracks. All three were 50- or 60-something CFOs with MBA and CPA credentials. They had all served as CFOs of significant companies and had decades of impressive experience. Not a slouch in the bunch. These are exactly the kind of people who are sought out for board work—people who can oversee the finance or compensation committees, for example. (Let's not get into to the dearth of women on for-profit company boards. Yes, progress to increase the numbers of women and persons of color are being made, but at a snail's pace. A topic for another time and place.)

> Three introductions from highly competent CFOs stopped me in my tracks: they were indistinguishable.

Back to the roundtable meeting... after hearing from all three men and dutifully taking notes as each spoke, I was stumped, and I told them so. You see, all of them sounded the same to me. Each of the three men listed all of the accounting and finance duties they oversaw. There were the meat and potatoes: accounts payable and receivables, monthly closings, interfacing with outside auditors, liaising with bankers and overseeing cash and debt; there was budgeting and forecasting and, to a man, the occasional higher-level executive work of preparing for a public offering, merger, or acquisition.

I explained to them that I was stumped because, judging from their introductions, they were indistinguishable. I couldn't possibly refer any one of them to a board opportunity I might come across because I would not know which of them to single out. They all sounded the same. I was instantly unpopular at the table, but they were too polite to actually throw anything at me.

Not unlike Karen, these executives were citing the table stakes of an accomplished CFO. What's more, Dennis McCuistion, our moderator and the Executive Director of IECG at the time, said that in a roundtable he participated in one day earlier, he heard from a woman who sounded just the same as the three men sitting with us. (I appreciated Dennis joining me as one of the unpopular kids that day.) There it was. Because my accomplished colleagues presented themselves as one undifferentiated professional, the only thing I remembered about them was their weird "three-ness" and not even their names.

The list method of introduction is pervasive in every profession and in every industry. Listening to software developers launch into their lists is probably the most painful, yet forgettable, introduction of all. It's like alphabet soup on steroids. I want to be respectful because it is people with these skills that make our world go 'round. I appreciate the work these geniuses do, but I worry about their ability to communicate with us mere mortals, especially upon a first meeting.

People coming from tech-
nology careers start listing the
technology, platforms, and
languages they have installed
or worked on. While it's a daz-

> List making is just a substitute for a real introduction.

zling display of the alphabet, it is useless for all but a few like-experienced comrades. For the rest of the population, it is not memorable at all.

Here is a profile summary example from LinkedIn:

> NET Framework 4.6+, .NET Core, APS.NET, C#, VB.NET. Utilized ADO.NET and SQL for DDL, DML, and creation of sprocs for CRUD operations. HL7 v2, HL7 v3(CDA), FHIR, and XML Interfaces to meet requirements. PE's services SAP system. Deployed an existing Java JAX-RS application. SQL Development, SSMS, SQL/Plsql

I didn't make that up.

Let me assure you that it doesn't have to be that way—even for the most technical among us. Later on, you will meet Mitra and see how this software developer introduces herself since crafting her Art of Hello.

List making is not a substitute for a real introduction. I have come to believe that many people speak in lists because, until now, no one has provided a better way for them to introduce themselves.

Keep reading, that better way is coming.

Now You're Remembered…Now You're Not

I met Shaunna Black in the summer of 2008. We were at a lunch meeting where like-minded executive women were launching an organization dedicated to helping women become for-profit board members. Iced tea was passed among us as we milled around the room. Since I was there to meet other business owners, I stepped up and introduced myself to Shaunna. Hopefully you know by now that I said, *"I am an executive recruiter and I fill hard to fill jobs."* She said *"I'm Shaunna Black, I help manufacturing companies become LEED certified."* Leadership in Energy and Environmental Design (LEED) is a popular green building certification program used worldwide, and Shaunna, with a degree in mechanical engineering and years of experience, was an expert in green manufacturing implementations. She had been a vice president at two massive semiconductor companies, installing LEED-certified manufacturing in plants worldwide. It was nearly a decade later when I realized that Shaunna had delivered a perfect self-branded introduction that summer day in 2008.

Our paths did not cross again until 2018. In January of that year, I was attending a lunch and learn business meeting, and there at the lectern was Shaunna introducing the speaker. After the meeting, I went up to her and said, "Hi, Shaunna, let me reintroduce myself. My name is Paula Calise. *I'm an executive recruiter, and I fill hard to fill positions.*" Then, I said, "Don't tell me. Your name is Shaunna Black, and you *help manufacturing plants become LEED certified.*"

Shaunna tilted her head and responded, "Wow, Paula, we haven't seen each other in a long time. How did you remember what I do?" I said, "Shaunna, as many people as I meet in my profession, I have never, never, never met anyone who said, '*I help manufacturing plants become LEED certified.*'" Without being aware of it Shaunna had crafted a perfect Art of Hello introduction in 2008, that allowed me to remember her a decade later. It was a satisfying moment for both of us.

Our conversation continued, and Shaunna shared with me that over the past ten years, her consulting practice had morphed and grown. "That's no longer exactly what I do," she said. "That's okay, Shaunna," I replied. "What do you do now?"

Shaunna gave me the long-form answer, slipping from one point to another providing me an updated picture of her as a consultant. I found I was having trouble connecting the dots, so I let her words slide in one ear and out the other, forgetting much of what she said.

This is not an indictment of Shaunna; as we've seen, this is how most people talk about themselves. Bits and pieces, lists, trying to wing it every time they find themselves answering the dreaded "tell me about yourself" question.

I find this a little odd. Each of us knows ourselves better than anyone or anything else. Still, the struggle to be brief and articulate about the product "ME" is universal. I have come to believe the difficulty stems from not having an actionable framework, some kind of easy-to-follow steps to rectify this gap in our professional arsenal. The gap can be filled with a simple, clear, and brief self-introduction that represents your professional brand promise. We all invest so much in our professional lives: education, training, and time trying to absorb the critique of others. We miss precious family moments, we lose sleep, we survive knots in the stomach, and yet we have not invested in finding a way to talk about ourselves that makes us memorable.

Shaunna's Archetype

If Karen's Art of Hello archetype is *The Biggest, Baddest Thing I Have Done*, Shaunna's is **My Newest Accomplishment.**

When I met Shaunna ten years earlier, she had just left Texas Instruments after a 20-plus year career where the last assignment she had as a vice president was taking the company's plants through the LEED certification process. She later used that skill and passion to form her own consulting business, helping many more companies move their manufacturing plants through the certification process. At the time, this was Shaunna's newest professional accomplishment. Thus, Shaunna's archetype is *My Newest Accomplishment*.

So far, you've met three people who have Art of Hello introductions:

Paula: *I fill hard to fill positions.*

Karen: *I revitalize tired brands.*

Shaunna 1.0: *I help manufacturing plants become LEED certified.*

There is something similar about these introductions. Let's dig deeper to find out what it is and how you can use it to develop your own personal brand introduction.

The Rules of Creating an Effective Art of Hello Introduction

In order to be *effective*, your introduction must be:

- Meaningful
- Authentic
- Unambiguous
- Differentiate you from others

Meaningful:

- Consequential
- Essential
- Important

- Purposeful
- Relevant
- Serious
- Substantial
- Useful
- Valid
- Worthwhile

> You own what you say about yourself and what others will mimic.

Meaningful sounds simple enough, but people get off track by making generic statements about themselves.

Example: *Driven, confident executive with years of experience.*

Ok, but what does this person *do*? For what industry and in what profession do they do it? What is their brand promise? Can't almost every manager and executive make the claim that they are "driven and confident" with "years of experience"? It is so generic that it lacks *meaning*. Putting meaning into every introduction is a promise of The Art of Hello framework.

Authentic: (This is the easy one: Don't lie—you'll be found out.)

- Accurate
- Authoritative
- Convincing

- Credible
- Legitimate
- Original
- Pure
- Reliable
- True
- Trustworthy

The second decade of this millennium was the "age of authenticity." To connect with an audience, a brand—be it a product or person—must be real. Eighty-six percent of consumers say that authenticity is a key factor when deciding which brands they like and support.[8] It's true for products and even more so with people. To be heard and liked, and to build advocates, a person's brand must be genuine and authentic.

Being authentic is the cornerstone of building trust. By trusting the authenticity of the introduction, we trust the promise it conveys and the brand deliverable of the professional. There are many writings on the lifelong exercise of building a brand. Here we see only the tip of the iceberg, the stated introduction—the brand promise.

> By having a clear and meaningful brand statement, you close down the opportunity for people to (mis)interpret your brand.

8 "Bridging the Gap: Consumer & Marketing Perspectives on Content in the Digital Age", *Stackla*, 2019, Retrieved on January 28, 2021 from https://stackla.com/ resources/reports/bridging-the-gap-consumer-marketing-perspectives-on-content-in-the-digital-age/.

Living the promise will be considered a given for the rest of this book. It's a must. Non-negotiable.

Stay tuned for a juicy example of an *inauthentic* introduction later when we meet Mike in Chapter Seven.

Unambiguous:

- Explicit
- Obvious
- Univocal
- Apparent
- Distinct
- Plain
- Unblurred

The issue I often find when I meet people and hear their introductions (or read them on LinkedIn or in resumes) is that people want to look good and important, but they haven't cited their real genius. That lack of recognition results in a statement like this:

> Experienced and versatile in multiple facets of management with extensive history managing business/service lines, teams, and projects for various clients and companies. More than 15 years' experience in delegation, overseeing, and management while exceeding goals and performance. Excel in uniting and motivating teams while helping them to achieve their goals. Effective leader and efficient delegator, a reliable team player with excellent communication, decision-making,

workflow, overseeing, and problem-solving skills. (68 words)

Sixty-eight words, yet I still don't know what this person does! I do not know their profession or their industry. And I am unable to remember the wordy self-description.

You own what you say about yourself and what others will mimic. In few places in life are you are in 100 percent control. But your brand statement—crafted, perfected, and repeated just the way you want it—is one thing you do have control over. By having a clear and meaningful brand statement, you close down the opportunity for people to (mis)interpret your brand. When you make vague, open-ended statements, people fill in the gaps and make their own interpretation of your brand— an interpretation with which you might not agree.

Differentiate:

- Discern
- Discriminate
- Separate
- Characterize
- Contrast
- Demarcate
- Individualize
- Tell apart
- Set apart

I love this one. Done right, your Art of Hello brand introduction sets you apart from others with similar professional backgrounds. And although I love this one, it is the one I get the most push back on from people who attend my seminars.

Your brand statement is unique to your experience.

I often hear: "But I do the same thing as everyone in my department." Or, "All controllers are alike; we all do the same thing." I beg to differ.

There are three reasons that people in the same profession can and should have a unique Art of Hello introduction.

- Reason One: Just by having a well-conceived Art of Hello introduction, you separate yourself from the pack. Easy peasy. Later you will see the results of polls I have conducted at my Art of Hello seminars. Thousands of audience members have consistently told me that they are aware of very few people who introduce themselves well, in a way that can be remembered. When you have an introduction that is clear, simple, and represents the essence of your professional life, you won't come across anyone else in your field using it. It will not happen.

- Reason Two: No two people have the same experiences. Whether or not you are in the same profession, no one brings the same personality and demeanor to the job as you do. You have different successes throughout your career than anyone else. These differentiators are represented in your Art of Hello brand introduction. *Your brand statement is unique to your experience.*

For Karen, based on her work at Mary Kay, *"I revitalize tired brands"* is her introduction. My friend Tracy Altman is, like Karen, a vice president of marketing with 20 years of similar experience. Yet her Art of Hello introduction is different from Karen's because her experiences are different. Tracey's introduction is *"I ignite brands and fans."* And she has the goods to back that up.

Tracey took a small regional product, once called AvoClassic—which sounds like an auto accessory product—and morphed it into a national brand, growing its revenue 100 times over, raising up avid fans, and making it the number one brand in its category. You may have heard of it: Wholly Guacamole! Tracey really does *ignite brands and fans.*

- Reason Three: You are unique. Everyone can have an effective Art of Hello introduction, but some don't because they lack the confidence to examine and then clearly state *how* they are unique. Beat down that fear of not being special and keep reading. No two people are alike. You *can* differentiate yourself.[9]* You must take the time to create

---

9   * There is a list of The Art of Hello branded introductions of people—some of whom are in the same profession—on page 189.

your own—your very own—Art of Hello introduction. In Chapter Ten, we'll walk through the
three simple steps for crafting your own.

Making Your Introduction (and Yourself) Memorable

We've just covered the important qualities (meaningful,
authentic, unambiguous, and differentiating) required
to make your introduction *effective*. But an introduction must also be memorable to be effective. Here are
the qualities you'll find in a memorable Art of Hello
introduction.

Clear and simple:

- Well-defined
- Sharp
- Obvious
- Evident
- Transparent
- Straightforward
- Uncomplicated
- Plain
- Unfussy

Simplicity is like *style*—it's hard to describe, but easy
to recognize. The antithesis of clear and simple (which
will be examined more closely later) is the convoluted
introduction scheme I call "MBA-speak." MBA-speak is
when a person uses all the sophisticated terms from their

graduate school days and strings them together to create an uncrackable code of gibberish. It leaves the listener thinking, "What?" Or worse, their audience takes the time to parse out the words, trying to create meaning, and ultimately, misses what's being said. MBA-speak is a built-in distraction.

I have collected many such introductions. (They're fun, so there'll be more later.) For now, here's an example of an MBA-speak introduction:

> Executive Leader with extensive domestic and international experience in operations, P&L oversight, multichannel product distribution involving both start-ups, growth organizations, and turnaround. Growing the bottom line while spearheading operational improvements that drive productivity and reduce costs.

MBA-speak at its finest. What does this executive do? Sales? Finance? Line management or staff? What industry? It's impossible to tell. Their introduction is definitely *not* clear and simple.

Brief:

- Short
- Concise
- Succinct
- To the point
- Condensed

Dictionary.com defines brevity as **the quality of expressing much in few words**. The Art of Hello effectiveness relies on brevity. And only brevity can make it memorable.

Brevity is the gold standard of effective introductions. Brevity is the real magic that allows your Art of Hello introduction to be remembered. It's short! In 1990, an advertising executive declared that in the year 2020, the average American adult would be bombarded with up to 5,000 messages every day.[10] It turns out he didn't foresee the explosion of online information gushing forth from all of our devices and underestimated the crush of daily content we encounter.

Lauren Totin, an internet marketing specialist, agrees:

> No matter where you look, you're likely to see a brand name not far away. And no matter what you search for, there's content on it. Thirty years ago, it was estimated that the average city dweller was exposed to between 2,000–5,000 marketing messages—and that was before the advent of the web as we know it.
>
> We can only guess at how many that number has grown to today, but if we account for the insane

---

10   Sam Carr, "How Many Ads Do We See A Day In 2020?" *PPC Protect*, April 9, 2020, Retrieved December 22, 2020 from https://ppcprotect.com/how-many-ads-do-we-see-a-day/.

growth of internet usage, we can guess it's likely much, much higher.[11]

You get the picture. Your introduction has a lot of competition for the space between a person's ears. The best Art of Hello introductions are ten words or less. I prefer six or seven words, and the fewer the better.

I had some fun researching what philosophers, writers, and pop culture gurus had to say about brevity. Here are some of my favorite quotes.

- **The more you say, the less people remember. The fewer the words, the greater the profit.**

  ~ Francois Fenelon, French Roman Catholic archbishop, poet, and writer

- **There's a great power in words, if you don't hitch too many of them together.**

  ~ Josh Billings, American philosopher and humorist popular after the Civil War

- **Some people talk too much without saying a lot.**

  ~ Mokokoma Mokhonoana, South African philosopher, satirist, and iconoclast

- **No weapons are more potent than brevity and simplicity.**

  ~ Katherine Cecil Thurston, Irish novelist

---

11 Lauren Totin, "Information Overload and The Future Of Marketing", *Teknicks*, August 6, 2014, Retrieved January 28, 2021 from https://blog.teknicks.com/information-overload-and-the-future-of-marketing#.W2TZ6dhKi2x.

- **When information is cheap, attention becomes expensive.**

  ~ James Gleik, American author and science historian

- **Brevity – the sister of talent.**

  ~ Anton Chekhov, considered among the greatest writers of short fiction in history

You be the judge of the effect of brevity. Let's take a poll: which of the following introductions are you most likely to remember?

1. *"I generate millions of dollars as a management and engineering consultant in international manufacturing disputes."* (15 words)

2. *"I turn manufacturing disputes into profitable outcomes."* (7 words)

Brevity must be learned. It seems that, as a species, we prefer verbosity. All of us have heard the adage, "A picture is worth a thousand words." Likewise, an Art of Hello introduction, done right, has the power to evoke many unspoken words of explanation.

> Brevity can make your introduction memorable.

Consider our next professional. Ellen's story provides another excellent example of the importance of brevity.

The first time I met Ellen, she spoke for about three minutes—a long time to listen attentively—about her job with an Ivy League school. She identifies companies in the southwestern United States that might be open to hiring her university's professors as consultants.

I was trying to follow her as she delineated the many academic specialties and higher education credentials of the professorial ranks, their past notable achievements, and a partial list of companies that have engaged them. At the end of three minutes, my head was spinning with impressive factoids about these esteemed academics. But the one fact that stuck out was that Ellen's monologue did not suit her goal: snagging more corporate clients. I stopped her and offered this alternative:

I make companies Harvard smart. (6 words)

Oh. Cool. Netted out, how much bang does Ellen get for six words? Invoking the name Harvard is definitely worth 1,000 words. Everyone knows about Harvard and can conjure up images of the smart, *smart* and exclusive university. To have access to that reservoir of knowledge is appealing. With this introduction, Ellen should have much less trouble getting the ear and maybe the first appointments she needs to be successful selling Harvard professors' consulting services.

I miss the TV series Downton Abbey—the classic tension and storyline of upstairs-downstairs, the richly written characters, the opulent costumes. But, mostly, I miss the crazy good dialogue. I particularly love the wonderfully sharp barbs of the Dowager Countess played by Maggie Smith. Her one-liners were brilliant ("What is a weekend?"). One of my favorite Dowager Countess moments was her declaration, "Nothing succeeds like excess," as she viewed the lavishly set Downton dining table piled high with silver, displayed to ensnare a rich potential benefactor.

> Simplicity is like *style*—it's hard to describe, but easy to recognize.

How is this opulent table related to The Art of Hello, you ask? Apparently, the same technique is at play when people grab the microphone to talk about themselves. Many people use lavish language in their introductions thinking that excess is impressive, and if they display everything they do, know and have achieved, they will snare attention.

How about this self-introduction I saw recently?

> I am a strategy, innovation and consulting leader with a pragmatic problem-solving sense to identify and strategically transform capabilities, business models, and value chains. With diverse and progressive global experience in strategy, business transformation, operations, P&L oversight, multichannel product distribution, digital ecommerce, partnership... (43 words and counting!)

The Dowager of Grantham may be right about the impact of a sumptuous, Victorian tabletop presentation, but excess doesn't bring success when it comes to introducing yourself. Our self-introductions must be simple in order to be useful to us. Short and memorable is always the goal. Ten words or fewer, preferably, that represent the essence of your professional life and define your professional brand are best. For establishing a memorable professional brand, "Nothing succeeds like simplicity." You can quote me—the *Dowager of Hello*.

Before we conclude this section, let me answer another often-asked question: How does The Art of Hello work for entrepreneurs, small business owners, or solo practitioners? People want to know how The Art of Hello can inform others about what they do at their own company where they may have many roles to play.

I understand the reasoning behind their question. As a business owner, I am the CEO and "chief bottle washer" of my company. I'm also the head of HR, Finance, Sales, and more. So, I have a complicated job in a lot of ways. But my Art of Hello is structured in the same way it is for any other person, business owner or not. It needs to answer the questions, *"How do I want to be known?"* and *"What is my brand promise?"*

For me, no matter which hat I'm wearing, I want to be known for that which grows my business and provides a revenue stream. I want to be known to the world as a person who *fills hard to fill positions*.

Don't overthink it. Ask yourself what you want to be known for, and then distill it. Whatever you come up with is your Art of Hello branded introduction. It doesn't matter if you own the company or if you're a small part of a company with thousands of employees. Get to the essence of your professional life and say it loud and proud.

The previous paragraphs bear repeating, so let me review (briefly)...

The best Art of Hello introduction is meaningful, authentic, and unambiguous. It differentiates you from others in your profession. It must be clear and simple and brief enough to be remembered.

It seems like a lot to manage in a few words, but it is very doable. I have created hundreds of introductions for professionals, and it has always proven to be worth the effort.

> Get to the essence of your professional life and say it loud and proud.

Earlier, we established that the long and boring elevator speech and the 30-second drill introductions are out, primarily due to the volume of information coming at us in such a rush that it decreases our attention spans.[12] So, now you have a decision to make: will you create a meaningful and memorable Art of Hello introduction or just continue adding to the noise that assaults people every day from every direction?

---

12 Adding to the noise: Totin, "Information Overload".

The Art of Hello Is *Your* Personal Brand Promise

Done right, your Art of Hello introduction is your **brand promise**. When Karen says, *"I revitalize tired brands,"* that is her brand promise to her employer. And when Shaunna says, *"I help manufacturing plants become LEED certified,"* that's her brand promise to the manufacturing executives who hire her as a consultant. For me, *"I fill hard to fill positions."* That's my brand promise to my hundreds of past, current, and future clients.

> The ability to be remembered is a valuable arrow in your professional quiver.

Here is a company brand promise definition I like:

> *A brand promise is a value or experience a company's customers can expect to receive every single time they interact with that company. The more a company can deliver on that promise, the stronger the brand value in the mind of customers and employees.*[13]

For personal branding, it would read like this:

> *A brand promise is a value or experience a professional's community can expect to receive every single time they interact with that person. The more a person can deliver on that promise, the stronger the brand value in the mind of his or her community.*

---

13 "The 5 Building Blocks of an Effective Brand Promise", *Workfront.com*, May 7, 2018, Retrieved December 22, 2020 from https://www.workfront.com/blog/the-5-building-blocks-of-an-effective-brand-promise.

Stating your professional brand clearly helps your customers (internal and external), business partners, colleagues, professional network, and your executive management team know what to expect every time they interact with you. You have established your brand.

And herein lies the secret sauce. If your brand promise (your Art of Hello introduction) is meaningful, authentic, unambiguous, clear, simple, and brief, it will differentiate you from others in your profession, and most of all, **it can be remembered**.

This is important: The ability to be remembered is a valuable arrow in your professional quiver. When your greater network can identify you in the same way you identify yourself, that network has the opportunity to act on your behalf even when you are not present. This is the basis for cultivating your career and professional advocates.

For decades we have been taught that a strong career is partially built on one's network—those who know you. It's even better to have supporters—those who agree with you. But the best is to cultivate advocates— those who act on your behalf in your absence.

The Payoff of The Art of Hello Introduction

A well-crafted Art of Hello brand introduction is the basis for people you are close to (and even those you may know only casually) to act on your behalf when you aren't present. You have, in essence, replicated yourself, making it possible for your brand to be in many places at one time. In meetings or social situations that you cannot attend, someone can easily bring you to mind when your talent or skills are called for.

A memorable brand introduction is important for career advancement. Imagine the hundreds or thousands of meetings that take place where the people in attendance are attached to key projects or are responsible for leading a team. They may be entering into a new business activity where a match between the business's needs and the staffing to carry it out are critical. Even if you are not there physically, you can still be in those meetings if a colleague from your network is there. They become your advocate. They are able to speak up about your talents, representing you at just the right time. This is huge. (This coin has two sides; the same principle is in play when people who have a reputation for being jerks get bad-mouthed and left behind.)

Fans for the Rest of Us

Earlier I suggested that as working professionals we seek to build our brands—not as celebrities do to build a fan base—but that is not entirely true. When you are not present, having an Art of Hello brand statement makes promoting you easy for your friends, colleagues, followers, and fans. Yes, though you may not be a professional influencer or pop culture icon, if you have consistently done a good job, completed work, advanced the cause, and treated people well, then you do have fans. These fans will speak on your behalf internally in an organization and at large, and they will do so positively if they know what to say about you. Your Art of Hello introduction makes it easy for your fan base to speak for you. You appreciate your network for acting on your behalf, and they, in turn, appreciate offering a sound referral or recommendation to their colleagues. It makes them look good. Win-win. But this can only happen when your network knows exactly what to say about you.

Track how many times a week you are formally or tangentially asked for a referral for someone with a certain skill and who is needed to move the needle for an organization, or to fill the need for a service that calls for a particular talent. I think you will be surprised how often it happens. Why? **Because good people always know good people.** A clear, easy to recite Art of Hello brand statement allows your colleagues, friends, and fans to refer you to career building, business building, and reputation building opportunities. My brand, *I fill hard to fill positions*, is so clear and easy that I have gotten new executive search clients with four degrees of separation. Create your brand introduction today and then use it every day; see what good things begin to happen.

Making the Most of Your Fan Base

The advocate opportunity is a real boon to anyone in sales or anyone building a company. Advocates simply refer business to you—and a lot of it. I'll use myself as an example.

I started my recruiting company in 2008 and all but stopped making sales calls a couple of years later because, by then, my network had taken over for me. Colleagues identified executive recruiting opportunities and sent them my way. It has happened for me hundreds of times, and it's because my brand—*I fill hard to fill positions*—is easy to remember and easy to repeat. And I fulfill the promise.

Here is an example of my advocates at work. One afternoon, I was driving to my Dallas office from a client meeting. My cell phone rang, and the Bluetooth took over, blaring the call inside the car's interior. When I answered, this is what I heard, "Hello Paula, my name is Cliff Orme. I am calling you from Costa Rica because I understand that *you fill hard to fill positions*, and I have a hard to fill position to fill." I had to pull off the highway to keep myself from causing an accident!

Later, I sat in my office and reconstructed the pieces of this amazing network-as-advocate business opportunity. Here is how Cliff came to call me that August day. Three weeks earlier, I attended a Dallas Business Journal function. Waiting for the event to begin, I struck up a conversation with a woman named Sharon who was an executive at an accounting services firm. We talked for maybe ten minutes at the most, exchanging niceties and business cards. I never spoke to her again. The following week, Sharon called on a CFO client, Leonardo, who described a problem his company was having filling a key position. They needed to fill it in order to achieve their strategic growth plan. Sharon told Leonardo about me—that I specialize in filling hard to fill positions—and provided my contact information. Leonardo in turn shared that information with Cliff Orme, the hiring manager for this international job assignment. Cliff called me and began the conversation using my exact brand language. Calling from Costa Rica, he repeated my exact brand introduction. Verbatim. *I fill hard to fill positions.*

> Your Art of Hello introduction makes it easy for your fan base to speak for you.

In marketing, this redefines brand reach! I call it amazing, and I attribute it 100 percent to my simple Art of Hello brand introduction: *I fill hard to fill positions.* I worked for Cliff and filled that position. Cliff is now my advocate; he has since referred another person who is seeking to fill a hard to fill position. Proof positive that the perfect Art of Hello introduction can gain business at four degrees of separation. In this noisy world, that is amazing.

Net this out: **done right, your Art of Hello introduction is your brand promise.** It is the core of your personal/professional brand. The community that wraps around you remembers you and your promise, then repeats it and represents you when you are not present. Career multiplication.

Building a network of advocates is enough of an incentive to create a great Art of Hello introduction, but let's go ahead and look at some other benefits of having an easy-to-remember professional brand.

- According to Wikipedia, personal branding is the conscious and intentional effort to create and influence public perception of an individual by positioning them as an authority in their industry, elevating their credibility, and differentiating themselves from the competition, to ultimately advance their career, increase their circle of influence, and have a larger impact.

- Ninety-five percent of recruiters say they view a personal brand as the essential differentiator between top applicants in the workplace.[14]

- Fast Company defines personal branding as, "You get to define how the world sees you."

Controlling Your Brand

There are very few aspects of our daily lives that we control 100 percent—how we define of our brand is one of them. (All this brand talk is of course predicated on the assumption that you always live out your brand promise. No bull, no exaggeration. If you say it, do it.)

14 N. Haig, "Your PERSONAL BRAND: Building a professional identity, and promoting it effectively, can be vital to an internal auditor's career," *Internal Auditor*, 75(1) (2018): 57.

Here is a simple example of control, or lack thereof. Let's say that I work in the retail sector, and I want to go on vacation. I can't just up and take off any time I want to, especially in November or December. So, I am not in control of the dates for my vacation. And there is more. Let's say one of my family members is a student, so I have to go on vacation during spring break or summer. Again, the control is not in my hands. But let's say my boss gives me the week of spring break off. Since my trip requires booking a flight, I find I'm still not in control—American Airlines is going to tell me when I can or can't travel in accordance with their flight schedules, not my personal preference. So, you see, even the simplest things, such as a date for a vacation are not fully in my control.

> Ninety-five percent of recruiters say they view a personal brand as the essential differentiator between top applicants in the workplace.

But when it comes to your brand promise, you're in control. The way in which you present yourself to the world is in your control through your introduction. You absolutely influence the way the world sees you. One of the very few things that you own in your professional career is your self-introduction, your brand introduction, your brand promise, your Art of Hello. Owning your own brand is a meaningful contributor to your success. The more clearly you can describe yourself, what you do, and the value that you bring, the easier it is for others to remember you. The super-saturated messaging world we live in makes it all the more necessary for you to cut through the clamor and deliver a clear message that defines your value.

The Value of The Art of Hello for Job Seekers

Job seekers will find having an Art of Hello introduction indispensable. First, it allows a person to know how to answer that awful but often asked tell-me-about-yourself question. This question isn't asked often by professional recruiters, but it is asked by hiring managers. And *they* are the ones who count.

Jack, an engineer by profession, came up to me at the conclusion of one of my Art of Hello presentations and told me this story. He had been unemployed for about seven months and was starting to give up hope of finding the right job. Three weeks earlier he had, in his words, "the perfect job opportunity, my dream job." He prepared well for the interview and when he got there, he was thrown a curve ball. Instead of meeting the hiring manager—as he was told he would—he was put on the spot with a four-person interview panel. They told Jack that they chose to interview him this way to save the managers' time and complete the interview process

> "If I had just met you three weeks sooner, I would be working at my dream job today."

in one sitting. Right out of the chute they said, "Tell us about yourself."

Poor Jack. He said he felt like a deer in the headlights: "I froze. I did not know what to say." Jack told me that the interview went downhill from there—and he wasn't surprised when he didn't get the job. Then, piercing my heart further, he said, "If I had just met you three weeks sooner, I would be working at my dream job today." The moral of Jack's story is not to miss the chance to have your dream job because you're not ready to "tell about yourself" with an Art of Hello introduction.

A second reason for job seekers to craft an Art of Hello introduction is that it informs their job search. Take Karen who we met in the opening pages of this book. When she and I hit on *I revitalize tired brands*, we didn't spend one minute talking about other aspects of her job search. We went right to work identifying the companies in North Texas that had tired brands. These were the companies that needed Karen's expertise. And her competition would not be so crisp in their value proposition (remember, the year was 2008, and a zillion marketers were vying for a few positions). With her effective and memorable introduction, Karen clearly had an advantage. Clarity is valuable for saving time and focusing professional efforts, particularly when searching for a job.

And then there is Elizabeth. Elizabeth contacted me after reading some LinkedIn posts on The Art of Hello.

She lamented that an important job interview had recently gone badly, and she now wanted to use The Art of Hello preparation for her next interview.

In a nutshell, she needed the perfect opening salvo that would answer the annoying question "Tell me about yourself." Once she had clearly stated what she does, she could follow up with one or two of her pillars—a short, prepared statement about her credentials and notable successes—delivered in one minute or less. You'll find, as Elizabeth did, that his simple yet powerful preparation will set you apart from many other job candidates.

I have spoken with thousands of job seekers, and I will tell you that many people are not competent to talk clearly about their core professional capabilities and successes. Having your Art of Hello introduction ready and then delivering some accompanying pillars with ease will allow you to stand out in a crowd.

The Jumping Off Point

At this point in my seminars, I begin hearing the number one objection to The Art of Hello: "Hey, I'm more than a 'one liner.'"

Yes, you are.

Whether you are just out of school or decades into your career, you've put time,

> The simple, clear, and brief Art of Hello introduction is just the jumping off point.

money, sweat, and tears into your profession. You have sacrificed nights and weekends at home with family and friends. You have given up enjoying the things that make life rewarding. Your career may have required you to travel at inconvenient times, to miss family functions, to spend time and money for continuing education, or to earn additional credentials. That mistress, "Career," is demanding. For all that effort, you should certainly be known by more than one line. More than just six to ten words should be awarded to you for the work and effort you've put into becoming the professional you are.

So, here is the payoff. The simple, clear, and brief Art of Hello introduction is just the jumping off point. The six to ten words—your brand promise—is the "hook" that allows people to know you, differentiate you from others, and then remember you and become your advocate. The Art of Hello introduction is the capstone statement—the top layer proclamation—of your professional life.

The Art of Hello® at a Glance

Chapter Three

We all deserve to be known for our achievements and to be understood for our value proposition.

- The Art of Hello Archetypes:
  - *The Biggest, Baddest Thing I Have Done*
  - *My Newest Accomplishment*

- Effective Rules for The Art of Hello Introduction:
  - Meaningful
  - Authentic
  - Unambiguous
  - Differentiating
  - Brief
  - Clear and Simple
- The Art of Hello is your brand promise
- People who know your brand become your advocates and fans
- You control your brand promise
- The Art of Hello is an important tool for job seekers

Chapter Four

The Bigger Picture of You:
Your Pillars of Strength

The Art of Hello introduction is the best way to get and keep the attention of your audience, but *pillars* are what you'll use to fill out your brand and acknowledge your accomplishments.

> *pillar* (noun): *a firm upright support for a super-structure.*[15]

The Art of Hello introduction pillars are additional support materials that fill out your professional brand. They are your credentials and notable successes that can be targeted to the audience you are addressing. Pillars

15 Merriam-Webster Dictionary, (n.d.) "Pillar," Retrieved November 5, 2020 from https://www.merriam-webster.com/dictionary/pillar.

can also be crafted as answers to questions you may anticipate being asked.

Most people are not prepared to introduce themselves properly. They spew disjointed information and flail around, grasping for an anchor to hold onto, not knowing what to say about themselves. This is when lists (remember Karen's mind-numbing litany?) or a bunch of sentences strung together without reason appear. I've heard them all. In the end, these unprepared self-introductions sound like blah, blah, blah, and trigger the listener's "so what" response. Poorly presented self-introductions cast a cloud of doubt from the get-go. They create thoughts like: *Is this person smart? Articulate? Focused?* or even, *Man, what a dope.* Talk about getting started off on the wrong foot!

Pillars to the Rescue

Pillars support and give life to the brand promise. They fill out your story; pillars give people more information about you. They are the stuff that you really want people to know about your skills, credentials, capabilities, experiences, successes, and aspirations. Here is where the arc and the details of your career find a home. I recommend that people craft three to eight pillars. Following are guidelines to create impactful pillars.

1. Highlight the important aspects of your professional achievements

Take a minute to parse out the top three or four areas of knowledge or experience a person should have to be considered an expert in your career field. For most of us, this is clear—it is the knowledge that we have concentrated on mastering to date. Even as a student, before years of accumulated on-the-job training, it is likely that classroom preparations are aligned with the deeper skills and knowledge that more tenured professionals have. The list of the core skills—or conversely—your specialty or unique skills and experiences are the starting point to crafting useful pillars.

Once you have defined the top areas of expertise for your profession, tag those as pillars. If you are among those who have used the list method to describe yourself, cluster the never-ending bullet points into categories and have something notable to say about yourself in each category. CPAs and CFOs are famous for using the list method to rattle off a vast number of tactical responsibilities they have mastered while climbing the career ladder to the top financial spot of CFO. It is a commendable and necessary attribute for the top numbers gal or guy to be detail oriented and want to be precise and complete in any work, including talking about themselves and their brand. So, to accomplish this without trotting out an ear-bleeding list of every piece of work singled out, highlight a few categories and say something impactful about each. For the CFO, this might mean including a pillar or two about risk management, financial reporting, banking or audit relationships and practices, revenue management, etc. Take the time to write out a sentence or two that highlight those professional achievements.

> Pillars are what you'll use to fill out your brand and acknowledge your accomplishments.

One at a time, build a small set of pillars that support the brand promise in your capstone Art of Hello brand introduction. If you are among those who have an elevator speech or a 30-second drill, it is possible that you have pillars already embedded in the diatribe. Dissect the 30-second drill and you'll probably find your pillars in there. Separating the pillars allows you the flexibility to use each one as the need arises, one at a time, whenever they are most useful. More on this topic coming up.

2. Highlight success stories

As noted earlier, a picture is worth a thousand words. Same concept here. One success story can paint a broad picture of competence. Find a few high points in your career that were particularly profitable or notable—perhaps they advanced the cause or just allowed you to shine—then write each of them in a format that can be easily told and understood. Some people like the STAR method which is an acronym for *Situation, Task,*

Action, and *Result*. STAR stories have long provided impact for job seekers during interviews. They work the same as a pillar of support to your brand promise. They are the *proof* that you are the person you claim to be, giving definition to your brand and assurance as to your authenticity.

3. **Develop answers to common questions and objections**

For example, if you are younger than most people of your career rank or level of expertise, and your Art of Hello brand promise seems too big for a person of your age, a pillar might sound like this: "I got started in this industry very young. Both of my parents are successful in the field, and I followed in their footsteps—beginning my professional training while at the dining room table."

In my case, when I tell people that *I fill hard to fill positions*, I often get the question, "What's considered a hard to fill job?" I have three stories I can tell that slip right off my tongue. I don't tell all three—I try to choose the one that my audience might relate to best. I know people will ask, so I am ready to tell.

> Be prepared. Think of answers to anticipated objections.

Any number of issues might become objections. Be prepared, don't dodge these questions, you know they are coming. Think of answers to anticipated objections in advance so you will own the direction of the conversation.

You know what you want to say, and, if you're ready, you won't get caught with your pants down.

4. Use industry jargon as a pillar, not an Introduction

Jargon can be a double-edged sword. The dictionary actually backs me up on this. It says that jargon is "the language, especially the vocabulary, peculiar to a particular trade, profession, or group."[16] That explains why people employed in the same industry easily communicate in the jargon familiar to them. But jargon is also defined as "unintelligible or meaningless talk or writing; gibberish." The words that communicate so well to others in your industry are gibberish to the rest of the world. If you throw in the second definition—you can understand why it's important to use jargon appropriately.

Industry jargon belongs in a pillar, not in The Art of Hello branded introduction. Period.

For fun, here are some synonyms for jargon:[17]

argot	vocabulary	doublespeak
idiom	abracadabra	drivel
lingo	balderdash	fustian
parlance	banality	gibberish
patois	bombast	insipidity
slang	bunk	lexicon
vernacular	buzzwords	neologism

16 Dictionary.com, (n.d.) "Jargon," Retrieved November 5, 2020 from https://www.dictionary.com/browse/jargon.
17 Thesaurus.com, (n.d.) "Jargon," Retrieved November 5, 2020 from https://www.thesaurus.com/browse/jargon.

newspeak	speech	shoptalk
nonsense	tongue	stale language
palaver	twaddle	street talk
patter	usage	trite language
rigmarole	cliché	hackneyed term
slanguage	commonplace term	mumbo jumbo

Some synonyms for jargon are respectable. Many require a step back. Do I want to load up my pillars with many terms that can be interpreted as abracadabra, drivel, double-speak, balderdash, nonsense, banality, bombast, gibberish, drivel, or mumbo jumbo?

This is meant only to be a warning. Use industry jargon in your pillars the way you would use Ghost Pepper Sauce on your eggs. Sparingly.

When Jargon Works Best

a. Tribal identification

Used with the right audience, industry jargon can connote *she/he is like me*. Used at the right time and place, it provides a very positive connection between people. It can form a quick bond with liked-minded people who share a profession or goals. Jargon that is used to make a tribal identification connects a person to a group or profession, fast.

b. Authority

A term of industry art, used properly and in the right setting, says, "This person knows what she or he is talking about." Knowing and using an industry term properly gives the impression that you have mastered the work.

c. Brevity

Jargon, used sparingly and well, can shortcut the need for a longer explanation. Always a fan of brevity, I think using jargon to communicate meaning in fewer words is perfectly acceptable.

d. Scripted and memorized

Your pillars, like your Art of Hello capstone, will be most useful to you if they are well scripted and memorized. Brevity is your friend in the world of pillars, as it is in the case of capstone brand introductions. Unless you are expected to deliver content, stories, or some element of entertainment—as when you are the sole presenter for an hour-long meeting—you are best represented when you are brief and articulate.

As for memorization, think of it like this. Bring to mind your very favorite TV sitcom. Although in reruns now, my favorite is still *The Big Bang Theory*. It's usually about 20 minutes of entertainment, with commercials filling the rest of the half hour. If you're like me, I adore the character of Sheldon because, as irritating as he is, he is 100 percent believable. And he is believable because he and the rest of the cast and crew have perfected every second of screen time through practice, practice, practice. Memorizing your pillars to the point of perfection makes them seem spontaneous. It's a conundrum of expertise—rather than becoming staid, the more you practice, the easier it gets to deliver your pillars naturally.

e. Used for internal meetings

It may sound awkward to use your Art of Hello introduction during internal company meetings where people from departments that do not ordinarily work on the same team come together. As good as it may be for distilling your professional brand, used internally or in your professional community, an Art of Hello introduction may raise eyebrows. Your co-workers already have an underlying understanding of what you do based on sharing an employer and its mission. Once a person is further identified by a work group or a department, The Art of Hello introduction, so useful in the world at large, seems just a little "off" when used with company colleagues.

Fear not. A pillar intentionally crafted for use inside a company or professional community can be helpful and durable. Here is an example. For years, I managed a large team of professionals at a Fortune 500 company. The company was addicted to meetings, from sunup to sundown. Many people on this team were subject-matter experts, so I would ask them to join me in meetings to fill in the details as appropriate.

At scores of meetings, I would introduce myself with my title and a short description of our responsibility or point of view on the subject of the meeting. The other people on the team would then introduce themselves. Inevitably, I would hear something like this: "My name is Chris James. I'm on Paula's team." Even as long as 20 years ago, I knew that introduction was wrong; I just didn't know why. On occasion, I would coach my team members, asking them to introduce themselves in ways that allowed their star to shine and give the listener practical information about their role.

Over time, we came up with some introductions that were definite improvements. Here are two of them: "I am Chris James, and I crunch the numbers for all new programs my team considers, looking for programs with the best ROI to bring to market." Another was, "I keep the master plan, schedule, and budget for all the programs that come from our department." In both of these cases, necessary context was added to the person's introduction. One was the team's Excel genius, the other was the budget guru.

> Jargon that is used to make a tribal identification connects a person to a group or profession, fast.

For internal meetings, using a pillar rather than your Art of Hello introduction makes better sense because it:

- Improves the introduction by being more descriptive
- Encourages team members to build their own internal brand reputations

- Makes meetings more productive because everyone knows each other's perspectives and expertise from the start

Pillars have various attributes that you can mix and match based on your audience. Here are some examples of pillars and how you might use them.

Your Credentials

Pillars will definitely include your credentials. This is where to showcase the MBA, CPA, PMP, CMP, PE, SHRM-SCP, CFE, SMAC, and so many more hard-earned credentials. Almost every profession or industry has advanced professional certifications that are coveted when achieved, and rightly so. These credentials are a badge of honor signifying that a person took their career achievement to the next level.

Resist the urge to include your credentials in The Art of Hello introduction itself— it is a hurdle to get over. In the examples discussed so far— Karen, Shaunna, Tracey, and me—none mentioned our credentials. Credentials belong in a pillar. They are not the definition of your brand, but they definitely support the authenticity of your brand promise.

> Credentials are not the definition of your brand, but they support the authenticity of your brand promise.

When your credentials are conferred by a prestigious source, that can be mentioned too. For example, if you have a Thunderbird MBA and are an international marketer, the two pieces of information go together like peanut butter and jelly, and they are just as sweet.

Your Company (or Organization), Named

A pillar is the place where you can include your company or organization. Naming your employer gives you a professional halo—especially if the company is a premier brand itself, well-known and highly regarded. If you are good enough to be employed by the top company in your industry, it reflects well on you. Again, naming the company (or organization) works for you when the company has a good name. An unknown company is irrelevant to building your brand.

As an example: "I've just completed my eleventh year with Boeing, now as the VP of Industrial Relations, after earlier completing my military career as Captain in Special Forces." (26 words)

Now that's a fine pillar! In just one pillar, this executive included his:

- Top-shelf employer (Boeing)
- Employment stability (11 years)
- Organizational status (vice president)
- Area of expertise (industrial relations)
- Past employer (U.S. military)
- Patriotism for serving (military career)

- Highly respected achievement (the rank of Captain)
- Underlying acknowledgment that his leadership skills earned him that rank
- Extra glow of a career in the highly selective Special Forces

This pillar communicates an amazing amount of information on the back of just 26 words.

Since *so* many people work for small businesses (there are 30 million small businesses in the U.S.) or lesser-known employers, using the company name can be a null event. For a long time, I may not have used the pillar with my company name in it because it didn't add anything to the conversation. Then in 2020, my company made it into the top ten on Forbes Best Executive Recruiting Firms list. At that point, it made sense to include this fact as a full pillar of its own. Now, I always state my company name, Linked, and bask in the glow of this extraordinary third-party endorsement. Still, I primarily care that you remember my name, and that *I fill hard to fill positions.*

The decision to use the name of your employer in a pillar is yours alone. Some people feel undressed without it, others don't. The question to ask yourself is this: Is my professional brand elevated by adding my employer's name to my pillar? Is it worth the precious little time I have in which to impart my brand to my audience? If yes, do it. If not, don't.

The Quantitative Pillar

Often, when beginning to understand the techniques for creating an Art of Hello introduction, I see people tossing numbers—generally big numbers—into their capstone statement. These might represent the revenue or percentage growth that a salesperson or a general manager has achieved, the money applied to advertising by a marketer, or the slimming of loss by a process engineer, etc.

> Just like The Art of Hello introduction, pillars should follow the rules of being simple, clear, authentic, and (relatively) brief.

Here is the general rule of thumb when including numbers: use specific numbers in your pillars, not in your Art of Hello introduction itself. As always, there are exceptions to the rule. Later in this book, you will meet my friend John who tucked a number into his Art of Hello introduction, and you'll see its impact. Pillars are very flexible in this way—they can accommodate any information you want to convey that further describes, supports, and explains your brand promise. Including the numbers as a pillar adds proof that you deliver on your brand promise.

Be sure to never use a term unless you can prove it, especially grandiose and financial terms. This is where you hold yourself to authenticity. When you have a solid number to use in a pillar, that's wonderful. Use it. For example, one of my pillars is that I have filled many hundreds of jobs. That's a good number. When I had only filled four jobs, as was true when I started my recruiting practice, I left it out. You can pick and choose the numbers that illuminate your brand promise. Do not add one that has any chance of diminishing your brand.

Making your pillars both *good* and *brief* takes time. Every pillar you use should be well thought out and scripted. A well-practiced pillar slips off the tongue and sounds so natural to your listener or reader that they might assume you just spoke about it for the first time, on the fly. That sound of spontaneity enhances your authenticity. *Authentic* not only means *truthful*, but it also means *heartfelt* and *sincere*—a great combination to be heard and remembered.

Just like The Art of Hello introduction, pillars should follow the rules of being simple, clear, authentic, and (relatively) brief. No use spending 100 words when 26 will do. The POW factor of the right 26 words is going to be greater than the impact of 100, unless you are a wonderful orator or have the genius of Thomas Jefferson scripting pillars for you.

Not Every Pillar Is Created Equal or Will Get the Same Wear

Once you have your corral of prepared pillars, you are set for prime time. You have your opener—your Art of Hello brand introduction—and you have pillars, prepared and memorized. Now what? This is the best part of the whole deal, I tell you. Now you use your arsenal to your best advantage in every situation. Open, and then choose the pillars that are most interesting or most likely to elicit a response from your audience. And the golden rule is that people are most interested in themselves. (You already know about asking questions to look smart, right? Yes, but that's a discussion for another time.) The audience and the circumstances of the encounter dictate the pillars you use.

> The pillars you use can (and should) be unique to different audiences.

For example, when I talk with a prospective hiring manager, I use this pillar: "I will fill that job the way you would for yourself, if you had the time." But, if it's the HR executive I'm speaking to instead I say: "I'm going to follow your internal recruiting processes when helping Lynn fill this position."

So, if I'm talking to the hiring manager, my pillar is: "I save you time." If I'm talking to an HR executive, I will remind them that I adhere to their recruiting practices, thus giving them peace of mind. In both cases I use pillars that are most likely to be of interest to the audience.

Of course, I don't use the same pillar in every single circumstance. I use my pillars as appropriate. I use my newer "Forbes proud" pillar when I engage with a very large company or organization. The bigger the company, the more prestigious it is to be hired to recruit for them. Yes, the Korn Ferrys of the world do have a huge advantage over my boutique firm in Dallas. But I still have that superb Forbes list endorsement putting me in the company of Korn Ferry, which was number one on the Forbes list in 2020. As the saying goes: it's the company you keep. As the principal and the head of my company, using my Forbes pillar puts me legitimately at the table of the HR VP of any premier client company. So, for a pillar, if you've got it, use it. Just be sure it is scripted and memorized.

Your LinkedIn profile is one place you may not have to be selective about the pillars you use. You can likely use all of your pillars. You have 2000 characters in the summary section of the profile. Also, your pillars can be imbedded into the jobs listed in your profile or in your summary. Go for it.

To recap, pillars are important because they round out your story. The pillars you use can (and should) be unique to different audiences. Have three, four, five, or six pillars that each highlight aspects of your work. Practice delivering them until they roll off your tongue.

There will be examples of pillars throughout the book, but for now, let's move on to the next archetype. This one requires you to take a look at your professional life with fresh eyes. Here's what can happen when you do.

Jennifer's Story

I met Jennifer at an Executive MBA meet and greet at Southern Methodist University. All of the EMBAs there were working professionals. Jennifer was a young woman, probably four or five years out of her undergraduate program. I approached her and introduced myself. Then I said, "Tell me, Jennifer, when you're not a student, what do you do?"

Jennifer answered my question, with her eyes on her shoes. "I'm a water engineer," she said. "I have a really boring job."

Whoa, let's not start there!

When Jennifer told me that she was a water engineer and that her job was boring, I did not have a frame of reference to understand that particular profession. Of the hundreds and hundreds of jobs that I have filled, I've never worked with a water engineer. In my mind, I thought that Jennifer might be the person who plans the flushing systems in tall buildings—I don't know!

So, I said to her, "Jennifer, I don't really know what that means. Give me a little information. What do you do?"

Jennifer answered, "Well, I work with the cities of Colleyville and Denton. And I work with Duncanville and McKinney, and I work with the HEB [Hurst, Euless, Bedford] towns." She continued, "I also work with Addison and Richardson." She went on and on listing North Texas towns.

"Wow, that's impressive," I replied. "But Jennifer, what do you *do*?" Same question, but I was hoping maybe the third time was a charm.

She said, "Well, I work with their data. I work with their populations and their population growth and trends. I work with their climate and microclimate information." She went on, "I work with their park land per capita, and I work with their water supply and runoff. I work with their percent of forest and wetlands."

Jennifer went on and on, her list sounding like tabs in a census report. By then, I had asked her several times to describe her profession to me, and I still didn't really know what it was that she did as a water engineer, so I tried one more time. "Well, Jennifer," I asked, "what do you do with all this information for all these towns and cities?" She put her head down and said, "I write their 30-year water plan so they can continue to grow and not run out of water."

Wow! That is not boring!

I thought about what she had shared with me and said, "Jennifer, if I heard you correctly, *you're an economic development professional, keeping North Texas growing by planning for water use for decades to come.*"

You know how Jennifer responded? She said, "Can I say that?!"

It was so charming, but also very naive. "Yes, Jennifer, you can, because it's truthful," I assured her.

Jennifer had been introducing herself using the title of the degree conferred by Texas A&M a few years earlier: Water Engineer. And she continued to think of herself only in terms of that title, even though her actual work product elevated the value of her contribution beyond that of any new water engineer straight out of college. She's an economic development professional, keeping people in North Texas in showers and stocked with iced tea for 30 more years! God bless her, love that woman.

Jennifer's Archetype

Young Jennifer had an opinion of herself that had become obsolete. But she moved beyond that simple "I'm a water engineer" to something better. The archetype here is *My Work in a Bigger Context*. Yes, Jennifer is still a trained water engineer, and, during the day, she still does the technical work of a water engineer. However, her impact on the world is now elevated to that of an economic development professional whose expertise is water use. That is Jennifer's work, placed in its *bigger context*.

John's Story

Tell me what you are proud of in your work.

I met John at an event. He was wearing a name badge, so I approached him and introduced myself. I said, "John, my name is Paula Calise. *I'm an executive recruiter. I fill hard to fill positions.* And yourself?"

John shook my hand and said, "My name is John. I'm a corporate real estate guy."

Of course, I knew he was a guy. That's not news. So, all I learned from John's self-introduction was that he was in the corporate real estate industry. No idea what he did or why he was special.

I don't know what made me ask the following question this way, but since that day, it has become part of my repertoire. I said, "John, in your corporate real estate career, tell me a point of pride, something you've done that you are really proud of."

John thought for a minute, "Well, when I was at Nike, my job was to do site selection." He said, "While I was there, I invented NikeTown."

John is a tall man. I looked up at him and replied, "Well, that's very impressive, but I'm not sure I know what that means. Tell me more."

So, he elaborated. "It was in the 1990s, and I found myself in Times Square in New York City," he said. "Times Square was not what it is today. It was seedy, there was graffiti everywhere. It was a little dangerous." He continued, "What I noticed was that many of the buildings that surrounded Time Square were empty or partially empty." He said, "Then, it came to me that, at Nike, we could take a lot of that real estate and display our merchandise; we could put up a handball court and display more merchadise. We could have a juice bar and a basketball court and have a merchandise display near by."

John is a very smart guy and somewhat of a futurist. In the 1990s, he was already inventing what we today call *experiential retail*. It didn't exist yet; that *term* didn't even exist in the '90s. John is an outpost thinker, right?

John went on to share with me that he took this idea back to his executives with a business case, with all the necessary marketing and financial backup. Nike leadership told him, "No, it's expensive. Why bother with this? It's not going to happen." John told me that it took him three years to sell-in the concept. He stuck to his guns and kept pitching his idea. At the end of three years, he was finally given the green light. Leadership told him, "Go and do a NikeTown, but do it somewhere where if it flops, there won't be too much notice."

I can't recall exactly the site he chose, but I do recall it was in Asia, maybe Hong Kong or Singapore. And John went on to describe the opening of the "superstore." He said there were people lined up around the block to get in. But even more important was that the international business press picked it up, and it was a sensation.

After that success, Nike approved and opened a total of six NikeTown locations around the world. Now that's a cool invention and a big innovation for a "corporate real estate guy."

I was impressed. "Wow, John, that is a great point of pride!"

And then he said something that surprised me more. He said, "You know what? While we're talking about it, if you don't mind, I could tell you another story."

I said, "Sure. Tell me another story."

John said, "Well, when I was scouting locations for Starbucks, I found myself on a highway in the late afternoon and felt like I needed a cup of coffee. I got off at the nearest exit. There was no Starbucks there, but I did find a McDonald's. I drove through and bought what was probably that morning's coffee." (This was a few years back, well before the McCafé concept—of course, McCafé has elevated McDonald's coffee to one of the best-in-class.) John continued, "So I drank this bad coffee, got back on the highway, and it occurred to me, *WOW, Starbucks can fill a need.*" Right there in the car that day, he envisioned Starbucks drive-thrus, something the company had never done before. So once again, John showed he's a good businessman. He went to the Starbucks executives and said, "I'd like to start some drive-thrus." He had a business case, marketing case, and a finance case.

How do you think the Starbucks executives answered? "No, we can't do that. We need our customers to come into the store. To be accretive to our brand, customers need to talk with the barista. They need to see that there's a live edge on the counter where the natural shape of the original tree is left intact. They need to experience our real leather chairs, hear the beans being ground, smell the coffee as it is served." John didn't buy

that. He said, "No, I really think this is going to work."
He went back, and he went back, and he went back again,
and finally, he broke through. Management said to him,
"Fine, you have the opportunity to open six stores with
drive-thrus." And they asserted, "Put them somewhere
that they will not be noticed if they fail."

Well, this was the second time he'd heard that. I can't
remember all the places where he said they opened their
first drive-thrus, but it seems that one of them was the
town of Franklin. I can't think that anything in Franklin
might be all that memorable, so it was probably a good
pick. John opened the stores, and a few months into the
experiment, it proved successful. The metric, *same day
sales*, in those six locations went up ten percent or more.
A ten percent bump for a retailer is huge; this was very
good news. John proved the success of Starbucks drive-
thrus. All of us who have used the Starbucks drive-thru
can thank John for his persistence.

After hearing these two awesome success stories, I
said, "John, what I'm hearing from you is that you're
in commercial real estate, and *you're a billion-dollar brand
builder on the back of old-fashioned brick and mortar retail.*"
John liked it right off the bat, and I like it too. Let's dissect this a little.

The alliteration of "billion-dollar brand builder"
with "brick and mortar" is good for memory. There
are a lot of Bs going on, and this works in John's favor for his Art of Hello introduction. Also, it provides

a counterpoint to our current commercial environment. There's nothing, nothing old-fashioned about Starbucks or Nike. These are some of our most stellar U.S. brands. But there's something old-fashioned about the concept of brick and mortar retail in contrast to the online shopping phenomenon sparked by Amazon and others. The mnemonic and social commentary make John's introduction unique and memorable.

> The mnemonic and social commentary make an introduction unique and memorable.

John's Archetype

"I'm a billion-dollar brand builder on the back of old-fashioned brick and mortar retail." I don't know if John is using that introduction today, but I certainly hope he is. The archetype here is **The Results of What I Do**. John's work gets results—he innovates and builds billion-dollar revenue streams for old-fashioned brick and mortar retail. Bless his heart.

The Art of Hello® at a Glance

Chapter Four

Art of Hello introductions are a jumping off point, and pillars fill in the gaps.

- Pillars highlight achievements, provide answers to common questions or objections, and are the correct place for your industry jargon

- Pillars can be mixed and matched — credentials, company (or organization) name, quantitative information — and used for internal colleague introductions

- Archetypes are formats that The Art of Hello introductions adhere to

  - Archetype 3: *My Work in a Bigger Context*

  - Archetype 4: *The Results of What I Do*

Chapter Five

What The Art of Hello® Is Not

By now, you've got a pretty good picture of what The Art of Hello is all about. And I think you might gain even more clarity if we look at it from an entirely different perspective: What The Art of Hello is *not*.

I have spoken before thousands of people who found The Art of Hello to be an indispensable tool they've been looking for to get ahead in their profession. Occasionally, however, there are those in the audience who have misunderstood or simply have questions about the process. I've compiled a list of the most frequently asked questions that come up in my seminars in case similar thoughts have crossed your mind while reading the previous chapters.

It Is Not Just a One-Liner

The reason it's not just a one-liner is because of pillars. Pillars flesh out the introduction giving additional information regarding your professional identity.

It Is Not an Advertisement for Your Employer

The Art of Hello is not an advertisement for your employer. You have met Karen, Shaunna, Paula, and Jennifer, and none of the four of us opened with the name of our company. (Actually, when I first met Karen she did lead with Mary Kay, but since it was her "before" introduction, it doesn't count.) If you want to use the name at all, I recommend that you use your employer's name in a pillar, as previously discussed.

> The rule is to use The Art of Hello brand introduction as your personal professional platform. Leave the business advertising to the business.

Let me give you an example of when using an employer's name does *not* work well. "Hi, my name is Larry. I work for AT&T. AT&T operates in 175 nations in the world. We have 250,000 employees, and we have the leading 5G technology, blah, blah, blah." Yes, fine, Larry. I pay the bills. I pay AT&T a lot of money. I know who they are. I still do not know who **you** are.

Still, never say never. You might want to use a company name in an Art of Hello introduction if:

- You are the founder, and it means the world to you; you just can't bear *not* to state the company's name

- You are the paid spokesperson for your company

- You work for a one-of-a-kind employer, such as a state or federal government agency that adds value to your brand, i.e., *Keeping America safe as an FBI agent*

- The employer's name adds value or color to your Art of Hello introduction

- You have a strong need to use your employer's name. If you simply must use the company's name, consider doing so in a pillar

These are the exceptions, not the rule. The rule is to use The Art of Hello brand introduction as your personal professional platform. Leave the business advertising to the business.

There was a time, however, when I did like the exception to the "no employer name" rule. I was conducting a workshop for a leadership development program for the Kroger Company. After the session, a man named Sam came up to me and admitted that he hadn't a clue how to brand himself.

After asking a few questions, this is what I learned. Sam was a superintendent for new store construction. He traveled the country to ensure that Kroger stores opened on time and on budget. In our conversation, I asked Sam what he liked most about his job. He told me that he liked meeting the local police who helped secure the building sites and materials, and he enjoyed meeting with the local fire chief to ensure that his store met local fire codes. He liked meeting the retail executives who would share the strip center with the Kroger store; he liked meeting neighbors who might be concerned about traffic, and he liked touring the about-to-be-open store with Girl Scout or Boy Scout troops. Not once did Sam mention drying cement, floor tiles, refrigeration, or even the timelines and budgets that he was charged to protect. For Sam, it was all about the people.

After listening to what he loved about his job, I said, "If I hear you right, Sam, you can honestly say, *I build communities by building Kroger stores.* Is that right?"

It made Sam smile, and he said, "Yes, *I build communities by building Kroger stores.*"

In this case, using Kroger's name does add color commentary to his Art of Hello introduction. We all know Kroger, the size, the product variety, the locations, the jingle they used in the past. The name evokes a richer mental picture than if Sam simply said, "*I build communities by building retail stores.*"

It Is Not Bragging

Another objection I hear in my seminars is that The Art of Hello brand introduction vaguely sounds like bragging. Why is it *not* bragging? It's pretty obvious: *It's not bragging because it's true.* Your Art of Hello is authentic. And if it's authentic, it's not bragging.

And there is another powerful reason why a well-crafted Art of Hello introduction is not bragging— because it's not about you *personally.* It isn't about how good *you* are, or how smart, successful, and rich *you* are. It is the opposite. An Art of Hello is about what you *deliver to others.* Think about the people we have met so far and their Art of Hello branded introductions:

- When Karen says, *"I revitalize tired brands,"* it's not *her* tired brand. She does this for her employer.

- When Shaunna says, *"I help manufacturing plants become LEED certified,"* she is not talking about her plant locations. She does this for her clients.

- When I say, *"I fill hard to fill positions,"* it's not about me. It's about what I deliver to my clients.

- When Jennifer says she keeps the water running, she does not mean just her water. Jennifer produces 30-year water plans for North Texas communities.

The Art of Hello introductions are brand promises. They are what people can expect from you when they engage with you. It is the opposite of selfish, the opposite of bragging.

Bragging sounds different. Bragging statements elicit the gag response. This is what bragging sounds like: "Hey, my firm, Linked, is in the top ten Executive

> If it's authentic, it's not bragging.

Recruiting Firms in the U.S. according to Forbes, and if you doubt me, come out to the parking lot, and I will show you my new Maserati." That sounds very different from an Art of Hello capstone or the pillars that support it.

It Is Not Everything You Have Ever Accomplished

The Art of Hello brand introduction, even taken together with the three to five pillars, will not represent your entire career. It is not meant to replace your resume. The capstone and pillars are meant to replace the crazy old elevator speech or the clunky 30-second drill. This means that, in order to have a great Art of Hello brand introduction and supporting pillars, you must make the hard choices to prioritize your most important accomplishments. Setting aside some parts of your career in order to highlight those that matter most to your brand promise is difficult. Accomplishments are hard earned. For me, it is like deciding at dinner whether to give up the bread and butter or the slice of pie. I have come to be attached to both. It's not fair, but it is right. Louise Brooks, actress and jazz age icon, said it well in regard to writing:

> *Writing is 1 percent inspiration, and 99 percent elimination.*

So, make peace with the fact that your Art of Hello is not everything you are or have done. It is the framework to be known and remembered, on which, over time, you can hang more evidence and details regarding your value.

> Prioritize your most important accomplishments.

It Is Not Lifelong and Permanent

Let's revisit Shaunna from Chapter Three. There is more to her story. During 2020, Shaunna and I connected via phone to work through how she wants to be known today. I heard her out. I heard the stories about her most recent successful consulting engagements and the clients who value her most. Shaunna, it turns out, had moved from the technical side—creating the nuts and bolts of process and procedural documentation, training and sustaining the LEED standards—to the leadership side, mentoring executives and helping them as a coach when they face difficult situations. Now Shaunna's consulting success revolves around being a sounding board, helping guide personal professional growth, shoring up managerial weakness, and bringing out the brilliance of the executives who seek her counsel. With this updated information in mind, Shaunna's Art of Hello introduction became:

> *Growing executive capabilities with head and heart.* Shaunna 2.0.

There is a lesson built into Shaunna's story. It is this: An Art of Hello introduction is not lifelong or permanent. It is how you want to be known *now*. This does not mean that I recommend making changes all the time, but when your career pivots or significantly changes, or when you eclipse the professional you were, or when you change professions entirely, that is when you change your introduction. As long as your introduction represents you well, don't mess with it. If it ain't broke, don't fix it.

> An Art of Hello introduction is how you want to be known *now*.

It Isn't an Asset Your Career Can Be Without

If you are pursuing career advancement, if you are a job seeker or could be someday, if you are in sales (it is commonly said *everyone is in sales*), if you are a business owner, if you are pursuing funding for a project or business, if you're a speaker or a blogger or just someone with something to share, then The Art of Hello branded introduction is for you. Anyone who introduces themselves in person or online deserves to have a professional brand that can be easily recognized, remembered, and acknowledged because it's a noisy, noisy world. If you have any chance or hope that someone's will remember you, you need a strong brand.

The Art of Hello® at a Glance

Chapter Five

What The Art of Hello Is Not

- Just a one-liner
- An advertisement for your employer
- Bragging
- Everything you have ever accomplished
- Lifelong and permanent
- An asset your career can afford to be without

Chapter Six

Payback:
The ROI of Being Remembered

If you are already, or somewhat, convinced that you want an Art of Hello introduction of your own, then this chapter puts the icing on the cake. If you are still unconvinced, just read this chapter and then make your final decision. If this doesn't do it for you, then shelve the book.

Besides reading as much or little of this book as you wish, I ask you to spend no more than one hour crafting an Art

> Invest one hour and get a durable and valuable Art of Hello introduction.

of Hello branded introduction of your own. One hour invested. That one hour has a huge ROI, maybe more than any other hour spent on your career this year, or any year.

By investing one hour, and many times it's even less that, you get an Art of Hello branded introduction that is durable and valuable.

Think about the modest six- to ten-word sentence you craft and its capacity to achieve the following. It can be:

- A one-of-a-kind asset in your professional arsenal
- A lead source, because people will remember and refer you
- The agent of your advocacy circle
- A way to introduce yourself that makes you memorable
- A tool that differentiates you from others

The same six to ten words are durable assets that can be used in many contexts:

- For in-person introductions
- On Zoom and other platforms for daily meetings
- At the top of your LinkedIn profile and in your summary
- To introduce yourself in the bio section of all social media sites
- In the executive summary of your resume

- On your business card, front or back
- As part of your email signature block
- On your voicemail greeting
- In your bio on your company website
- Anywhere you want to be seen and known for your professional achievements

Your brand statement and Art of Hello introduction will be used again and again and again and again and again. The ROI of an hour spent creating such a statement is astronomical. I've used mine 10,000 times, maybe 100,000 times, who knows. Additionally, it is the exclusive tool that powers my source of business leads—with over ten years of success. Wow. What an ROI for an hour spent crafting it! Amazing. I ask you, what other way can you spend one hour that has that kind of return for your career?

The ROI from having a well-crafted, authentic, impactful, and memorable personal brand introduction is enormous. Here is one way to think about it:

> What if you were intentional with your professional brand and made it ready for prime time?

Every single day, you get ready to present yourself to the world. Before you go to work or school, a civic meeting, a dentist appointment, or wherever your destination may be, you shower, brush your teeth, manage the mane, select clothing, dress, and check your reflection.

On weekends, you may have a similar routine, but perhaps with a more casual goal. It takes at least 30 minutes, maybe more, for most of us to get ready to show ourselves to the world. Do the math. Thirty minutes a day, 365 days a year. That's a whopping 182 hours per year spent making ourselves presentable.

The physical appearance we present—our clothing and grooming—is expensive in both time and money, and yet, we would have it no other way. We are who we present ourselves to be. We have a lot tied up in our image, and as professionals, we bought into the idea early to dress for success.

What if you were as intentional with your professional brand, making it ready for prime time? The good news is that it only takes one hour to make your professional brand ready-for-prime-time presentable. The Art of Hello introduction represents you and says as much about you as the most glamorous or dapper ensemble. Craft The Art of Hello branded introduction and put it to use, earning you the ROI your time deserves. Use it in all venues and put it to all uses, consistently. The ROI from one hour spent honing your personal brand introduction is astronomical.

The Art of Hello® at a Glance

Chapter Six

The ROI on a Well-Crafted Art of Hello Introduction Is Huge

- This modest six- to ten-word sentence can be:
  o A one-of-a-kind asset in your professional arsenal
  o A lead source because others can remember it and refer you
  o An agent of your advocacy circle
  o A way to introduce yourself in a memorable way
  o A tool that differentiates you from others

Chapter Seven

Memorable Stories
with The Art of Hello® Impact

Without the examples of those who have successfully used The Art of Hello to promote their personal brand, it's hard to imagine its power. That's why I've included several of their stories. Here are the people we've met so far and their Art of Hello introductions:

- Karen - *I revitalize tired brands*
- Shaunna - *I help manufacturing plants become LEED certified*
- Paula (me) - *I fill hard to fill positions*
- Jennifer - *I am an economic development professional. I keep North Texans in water for decades to come*

- John - *I am a billion-dollar brand builder on the back of old-fashioned brick and mortar retail*

Let's meet a few more of my friends, hear their stories, and learn about the archetypes that characterize their Art of Hello.

Mike's Story

Let me introduce Mike. I met Mike at a business meeting, and he introduced himself this way, "Hi, my name is Mike. I'm a financial advisor, and I help get people over their financial finish lines." Oh, I like that. Right? "I get people over their financial finish lines." It gives you a visual impression of a sports competition, with the winner getting to the finish line first. In swimming, I imagine a picture of a swimmer touching the wall; in track, it's breaking the tape. This introduction is a clear metaphor for success. I like the positive mental image and the glow of an introduction where a few words are worth 1,000, which Mike's introduction accomplished.

Shortly after the meeting, Mike and I met for coffee. After the niceties, I opened with this question, "Mike, to get to know you and what you do, tell me a few stories about clients who love the work you do for them and would refer you to their friends."

> A person can't hide behind a tag line for long if the brand promise doesn't match what they actually deliver.

Mike shared six stories of clients who appreciate the guidance he has given them.

He thought a little more and said, "Well, one of my clients that I just adore is a retired schoolteacher. I met her about 18 months ago, right after Christmas. She came into my office and told me she was 'living close to the bone.'" She was concerned about the possibility of outliving her teacher's pension and having to rely solely on her social security income. She told Mike, "I'm afraid that I'm just going to be destitute."

She also disclosed that she hadn't been able to see her grandchildren at Christmas that year because she didn't have the money for a flight. "I didn't even buy them presents," she said, "because I just didn't have the money. So, I put a $10 bill in a card and sent it to them, and that was it."

Mike said it was heartbreaking to see her living this way after having dedicated her life to teaching. He went on to tell me that after spending some time with the retired teacher, he found out that her situation was not nearly as dire as she thought it was. She had just never been a good money manager, she hadn't learned, as she was busy dedicating her life to her students. She didn't understand investments. So, Mike created a financial plan for her.

Mike told me he visited with her again the following year. She said to him, "Mike, I want to tell you, I saw my grandchildren this Christmas. Because of you, I knew I had the money to spend on airfare, and I took them all presents."

Mike's story warmed my heart; he had made a real difference in that woman's life.

Mike went on to tell me about a client who had twin daughters who were in the tenth grade. When Mike first met this man, he looked as if he was carrying the weight of the world on his shoulders. He explained to Mike that, try as he might, he was sure he wouldn't have enough savings to send both of his girls to college without them taking on student loan debt. He knew taking on that debt might burden the girls for decades to come.

Mike worked with the whole family and helped broker an agreement between his client and his daughters that would help their financial future. If the girls would agree to take their freshman year at the local community college, Dad could cover the rest of their undergraduate education at a state university—allowing the girls to be debt free. All three agreed to the plan. Mike helped that family—not just his client, but the next generation as well.

Mike shared additional stories of the clients he served who he believed liked him enough to refer him to other potential clients. He told me how he solved an ongoing rub between a couple with divergent investing preferences; about a young adult who had a desire to save for the long term, yet still wanted to buy a car now. He told me about first-time investors as well as seasoned investors he had helped.

I took careful notes as Mike told me his favorite client stories. When he was finished, I reviewed what I had heard and said, "Mike, I appreciate how much you like these clients and how much they like you. I do have an observation. Not in a single case did any of your clients 'get over their financial finish lines.' Not one retired at 40. No one lived their dream and bought a condo on the beach in Maui. Not one bought a classic car from Jay Leno." That doesn't mean Mike wasn't good at his job. He was. He really helped people. But through his stories, I learned that Mike really didn't deliver what his personal brand introduction promised.

Mike's Archetype

"Mike, I heard you telling me through your stories that you *help clients become comfortable and confident in their financial futures.*"

You see, Mike is a guy who listened well, who was empathetic, who helped people and brought them through the process of being better investors slowly, so they felt comfortable and confident. Mike's archetype is *The Essence of Who I Am*. You see, Mike was the kind of guy who, if he hadn't chosen to be a financial advisor, could have been a nurse, a psychologist, or a pastor. He was a caring person, one who listens and helps people solve problems and take financial actions that help them feel comfortable and confident in their financial futures.

Mike's *real* brand promise had nothing to do with financial finish lines, the wall touches, winning by a nose, or any other images that conjure up winning, succeeding, or beating the competition. To say that he put people over their financial finish line came across as disingenuous. It sounded good, like a marketing tag line would, but it was not authentic. By saying, "I help people get over their financial finish lines," there is a problem. None of his clients would say that about him because that was not their experience. However, these clients might call a friend and say, "Hey, if you ever need a financial advisor, give my guy Mike a call. He always makes me feel comfortable, and he's given me confidence in my financial future."

Authenticity is a core value of The Art of Hello. If an introduction is inauthentic, it shows. A person can't hide behind a tag line for long if the brand promise doesn't match what they actually deliver. Once their brand is found to be a fraud, the person's network will not embrace them because they have lost their credibility.

As we discussed earlier, a real benefit of having a well-crafted and authentic Art of Hello brand introduction is that your network becomes your advocacy squad, acting on your behalf when you can't be present. No one wants to speak on behalf of a person espousing an inauthentic brand. Inauthenticity is corrosive.

I have no idea if Mike is using his more authentic Art of Hello brand introduction. Maybe he stuck with the sounds good but it's phony tagline, but I hope not.

A Look at the Successful *The Essence of Who I Am* Archetype

The archetype I call *The Essence of Who I Am* can be applied to people in any profession. Take Warren and the buttoned-up world of accountancy.

I knew Warren as a senior financial executive, an MBA, and a CPA. While on a job search, he described himself in the way many thousands of others in his field do: financial controls, reporting, analysis, error detection, banking relationships, audit, cost savings, standardization, revenue gains, and on and on. The problem is that, again, those tactical experiences are table stakes for C-suite financial executives. After I spent a few minutes uncovering how Warren achieved his significant and sustained professional wins, it became clear that Warren was not the run of the mill financial executive, he was different.

Warren *drives financial improvements through the people side of the business.* He looks at organizational design and processes, as well as assessing the health of an organization, to create financially profitable solutions. As talented and accomplished as Warren is with numbers, he has learned (and has the instinctive tendency) to look to people—their behaviors and the processes they have built—to find financial improvement opportunities. Warren fills this valuable role every time he enters a new business operation because it is the essence of who he is. He's a people guy in an accountant's clothing. Today, Warren's Art of Hello introduction is *I drive financial improvements through the people side of the business.* Good guy to have on the team, no?

Bill's Story

Let me introduce Bill Wallace, my friend of about 25 years. I am in good company. Countless people in North Texas and beyond know Bill and call him friend. Bill runs an organization called Success North Dallas. Since 1988, Success North Dallas has brought topical speakers to its lectern, providing hundreds of people each month the opportunity to meet new colleagues and old friends, while enjoying career-enhancing networking (it's a "who you know" world).

Bill, who has been organizing and hosting these meetings the entire 30 years, says this about himself:

> *"I introduce the right people, for the right reasons, at the right time."*

Bill Wallace has been saying that about himself for 30 years. It is his brand, and he is known for his generous and spot-on introductions of friends, colleagues, and business acquaintances. Bill is an example of how powerful an introduction can be.

I conducted an Art of Hello presentation for a leadership development program at the company Epsilon. About three weeks after that presentation, I received a call from my friend who worked for Epsilon at the time and had been in the audience that day.

When she called, she said, "Paula, guess who I met today?"

"I don't know. Who did you meet?" I asked.

"I met Bill Wallace this morning."

"Very good, I am glad to hear it!"

"Listen how it happened." She said, "I was in a meeting, and I had my back to someone." This man says, "*I introduce the right people, for the right reasons, at the right time.*"

My friend went on, "I swung around, looked him in the eye, put my finger on his tie, and said, 'Hey, I know you! You must be Bill Wallace.'" Of course, Bill said, "Yes."

> Be consistent and you'll be instantly recognizable.

Then she exclaimed, "Paula Calise told me you would say that about yourself!"

As that story illustrates, you don't even have to be looking at a person for their brand promise to identify them. When their brand promise, their brand attributes, and their brand statement is so clear that it identifies them, that is perfect.

Bill's Archetype

The archetype for Bill is *My Repeated Successes.* Over the decades that he has run Success North Dallas, Bill has introduced hundreds and hundreds and hundreds of people to each other *for the right reasons at the right time.* That is a beautiful Art of Hello introduction.

Christina's Story

I want to introduce you to one more person. Her name is Christina. I was presenting The Art of Hello in a two-hour format, an hour of presentation and an hour of workshop, where the audience was paired off to work on their own Art of Hello introductions. During the workshop, I noticed Christina shaking her head. She seemed to be struggling. Clearly, it was a troublesome exercise for her, so I said, "Christina, either you're not buying this, or it is hard for you. Please tell me what's going on."

Christina responded, "Well Paula, I don't want to be known for what I do during the day."

I didn't really understand what she meant until I sat down and listened to her story.

You see, Christina paid the bills with her technology sales career, but her real *passion* was being an advocate for organ donation. In my conversation with Christina that day, I learned the reason for her passion. This lovely young woman had donated a kidney to a stranger so that person could live a full life. How wonderful is that? After hearing her story, this is what I crafted for Christina that day:

> *"By day, I sell cloud technology, and by heart, I advocate for organ donation."*

Christina's Archetype

I call this archetype *My Aspirations*. "My Aspirations" introductions have two parts, a *this* and a *that*. This is the type of introduction used when a person is a student, about to change careers, about to seek a job, or has a driving passion or avocation that is not their day job.

When I present The Art of Hello to MBA students and law school students, the aspirational introduction is the archetype we usually come back to. It allows a person to claim two positions—the first is usually what they are doing right now (student, job seeker, etc.), and the second declaration is their heart-story or what they are becoming. One of my favorite examples of an aspirational Art of Hello introduction is this from a law school student:

> *"My Aspirations" introductions have two parts, a this and a that.*

> *Working on a law degree in order to help clients win high-stakes cases through the Art of Advocacy.*

Archetypes Recap

Archetype 1. *The Biggest, Baddest Thing I Have Done*
Example: Karen - *I revitalize tired brands.*

Archetype 2. *My Newest Accomplishment*
Example: Shaunna - *I help manufacturing plants become LEED certified.*

Archetype 3. *My Work in a Bigger Context*
Example: Jennifer - *I am an economic development professional; I keep North Texans in water for decades to come.*

Archetype 4. *The Results of What I Do*
Example: John - *I am a billion-dollar brand builder on the back of old-fashioned brick and mortar retail.*

Archetype 5. *The Essence of Who I Am*
Example: Mike - *I help my clients become comfortable and confident in their financial futures.*

Archetype 6. *My Repeated Successes*
Example: Bill - *Introducing the right people, for the right reasons, at the right time.*

Archetype 7. *My Aspirations*
Example: Christina - *By day, I sell cloud technology, and by heart, I advocate for organ donation.*

The Art of Hello® at a Glance

Chapter Seven

- Archetype 5 - *The Essence of Who I Am*
  - Mike's lesson is to avoid a catchy tagline if it's not truthful. Instead, identify the essence of who you are as a person and use that as the basis for your Art of Hello introduction.

- Archetype 6 - *My Repeated Successes*
  - Bill's story highlights that his repeated successes are the distillation of his professional life, and they are the basis for his Art of Hello introduction.

- Archetype 7 - *My Aspirations*
  - Christina demonstrates that an Art of Hello introduction can be a glimpse into a preferred future or a personal passion.

Chapter Eight

Avoid the Classic ~~Errors~~ Mistakes

The best way to craft your own Art of Hello branded introduction is to avoid the errors.

Growing up in my hometown, we were baseball fans. Living in the no-man's land of Connecticut, you followed either the Yankees or the Red Sox. I lived in a family divided, which was a lovely way to have it both ways. My Dad would hike me up to Boston, and we would sit in the $2 seats near Fenway Park's big Green Monster. I saw Carl "Yaz" Yastrzemski play. And when my uncle would take me and my cousins to the old Yankee Stadium, we kept him so busy shelling peanuts, he would hardly get to enjoy the game. Good memories. It was then that I leaned about errors.

> Wikipedia says: In baseball statistics, an error is an act, in the judgment of the official scorer, of a fielder misplaying a ball in a manner that allows a batter or baserunner to advance one or more bases or allows a plate appearance to continue after the batter should have been put out.

The Art of Hello introduction is the distillation of your professional work and how you want to be known.

Fancy way to say *a mistake.*

Self-introductions are rife with mistakes. Examine these mistakes so you can put them aside and craft your Art of Hello cleanly.

All of the *how-to's* to create your Art of Hello impactful introduction are laid out in Chapter Ten in three straightforward steps.

Skippable Mistakes When Crafting Your Art of Hello Branded Introduction

- The List Method
- Chronological Introductions
- MBA-speak
- Your Job Title
- Your Degree Name
- Inconsistency

Skippable Mistake #1: The List Method

By now, you can now easily recognize the list method of introduction. We know it from Karen's story, the first person we met. You recall how Karen opened the conversation with me:

> I have done events. I've done collateral, I've done all kinds of research, qualitative research, quantitative research. I've done promotions. I've done online work, social media, website promotions, landing pages, supervised SEO and SEM projects, and more. I've worked with the consulting sales force. I've worked with executives on public relations, and I've worked with them on crisis communications. I've worked with product developers on color theory, packaging, and labeling information. I've studied consumer and sales behavior, imbedding that into marketing plans...

Citing a list of tactical accomplishments, skills, or projects in an introduction is very common; however, it doesn't serve the person well.

Three things are likely to occur when the list method is used as a substitute for a well-crafted and impactful introduction:

1. The "so what" meter flicks on. As a listener, when Karen is droning on and on and on, in my head, I heard *so what? so what? so what? Who hasn't done those things as a vice president of marketing?* The person is

diminished right off the bat in the mind of the listener. Instead of demonstrating professional breadth, they are making themselves sound like everyone else. If there is something extraordinary on the list, it may not be heard because the listener already labeled them as ordinary.

2. Worse yet, the listener (or reader) zones out completely. They may pretend to be listening, but you just can't tell. The point of any introduction is to establish a relationship, but by employing the risky list method, it's very likely that any opportunity for further acquaintance is shot.

3. A list method introduction is a well-worn path to being forgotten. Lists are heard all the time sparking the "so what" switch or "open eyes, closed ears." If the point of being introduced is to encourage mutual work or create a professional relationship, it is counterproductive to start wrongly.

This *too much is too much* concept is especially true when the information listed is the same for every other professional in your field.

As tempting as it is to prattle on about the work you have done and can do, please stop yourself and move some of these accomplishment to the pillars. Remember that The Art of Hello introduction is the distillation of your professional work and how you want to be known. This is your brand and brand promise. Dodge the bullet of list making, no matter how tempting.

Skippable Mistake #2: Chronological Introductions

I attended a small meeting with three other people: a not-for-profit board member colleague and two executives from a company that we hoped would sponsor an event we wanted to host. Let me set the stage for you. The four of us sat at a square table, one person on each side—a good seating plan for a lunch, not so great for a business meeting with four people representing two constituents. Rather than sitting next to each other, as I would have preferred, I was sitting across from my colleague.

I opened the meeting by introducing myself briefly, stating the purpose of the meeting, and thanking the two executives for meeting with us. Next, my colleague jumped in to introduce himself, and my immediate world began to unravel.

> A resume is not an introduction. A resume is a resume.

He started by saying, "My technology career is long. I graduated from college in 1980 and took my very first job in technology, working for the XYZ company. I stayed ten years before joining a competitor, the ABC company, in 1990. In 1993, I moved from the development side to the technology sales side and thrived at a sales career at both XXX and YYY companies for the next ten years. More recently, I moved to a professional association as the membership director and liaison to the technology community here in North Texas..." and he went on.

I was getting dizzy listening to him. In that moment, I was sure that our quest to enlist these executives to invest in our event was squashed. I made eye contact with my colleague and made the "knife cutting my throat" gesture, begging him with my mind (and metaphoric knife slit) to shut up. Since the executives were looking at him and not me, I don't think I was seen.

My colleague didn't immediately end his personal introduction. Instead, he hastily brought us up to date to his current role, and then thankfully stopped talking. In spite of his verbosity, good progress was made that day, and the executives' company sponsored our event.

But, YIKES! "I started my technology career in 1980…" A technology career in 1980? Really? Not quite up-to-date skills, I would say. You might as well say, "My first cousin is a tetradactyl."

A resume is not an introduction. A resume is a resume. It's there for interested parties to read, not something to be hoisted upon innocent new acquaintances. No one can remember the details of dates, titles, and companies strung together in a long introduction.

As a recruiter, I receive unsolicited emails of introduction nearly every day. People in job searches want to introduce themselves to executive recruiters in hopes of being top of mind for an open position. Recently, I received this email. I blanked out the names of the companies to protect this poor man's identity:

I worked for 20+ years in the software industry. I started off programming ERP systems - and quickly moved into software consulting for XXX Systems - a provider of wholesale distribution solutions throughout North America. When given the opportunity to move into sales in 1998 I moved to New York City to begin selling solutions to new accounts. I was a top performer for many years with XXX. In 2005 I moved back to Texas and began selling solutions to Large Enterprise sized companies in the Southern US. I have worked with many organizations over the years and strive to provide them with tools that can help improve their operational efficiencies, optimize inventories, improve margins, and increase revenues. I strive to be highly ethical and straight forward with the companies I work with - companies like XXX Supply, XXX Machine, JXX, RXX, United XXX, DXXX, XXX Distribution Group, HXX, Standard XXX, GXXX, Inc, XXX Global, XXX Enterprises, Century XXX, IXX Distribution, WXX, BXX Industrial, BXX, LXX, and more then [sic] 100 other companies. In 2014 I moved on from EXXX and joined forces with WXX - THE leading mobile/cloud based unified solution for financials and human capital management. WXX started with a "blank sheet of paper" in 2005 and has built some incredible systems for your business. In 2016 I moved over to KXX to run our XXX alliance in the Southern United States. I focus on helping our clients and partners understand the value of the cloud in transforming their HR and Finance operations. To find out how I can help you please reach out to me anytime at XXX.com, call/text me at 972.XXX.XXXX, or tweet me @ ixxxxx.

I couldn't make this up if I wanted to.

That email is a perfect example of what is wrong with a chronological introduction: it creates cognitive overload which causes the listener to tune out quickly. Krystal Overmyer, a journalist specializing in digital marketing trends, posits that *cognitive overload* can be overcome by focusing on the quality of your content.[18]

The chronological introduction cannot represent your brand. All it says is that you have an employment history. The points of pride and successes are missing or drowned out. Your professional brand is the essence of your professional accomplishments and how you want to be remembered—it is not your census data.

Skippable Mistake #3: MBA-Speak

Perhaps the most common mistake people make is by introducing themselves with a string of sophisticated business terms that are the hallmark of an MBA program. I

---

18 Jonathan Crowl, "Don't Have a Marketing Data Scientist? You Don't Know What You're Missing," *Skyword*, April 19, 2018, Retrieved December 22, 2020 from https://www.skyword.com/contentstandard/marketing/why-information-overload-shouldnt-be-a-big-marketing-concern.

believe many people are lured in by this style of introduction because they think it makes them sound smart.

> If you want to be remembered, MBA-speak is a deal killer.

Here is an example of MBA-speak that I found on a LinkedIn profile: "I am the strategic integrator who is the liaison between global operations and partners development."

It looks like a bunch of words from an MBA program squished into one sentence. What does it mean, and who can remember it? For fun, I re-wrote the claim by scrambling the words: "I am the development integrator who strategically partners with liaisons in global operations." And, "I am the liaison to global operations building strategic relationships for integrated operations." Any way you shake it, MBA-speak is a mistake.

Look at this introduction for a similar example:

> "As a CFO, I help firms accelerate profitability and improve their operational efficiency."

It is a mouthful. There are five sophisticated words for the busy listener to digest. Accelerate, efficiency, improve, operational, and profitability. The problem is that all the words are individually understandable, but when strung together, it takes a second for the listener to assemble and interpret the meaning. You can only hope that the interpretation matched the intended meaning. Not only is contact lost momentarily, but there is the risk

> For a person to act on your behalf when you are not present, your brand must be clear as a bell.

that your intended meaning is no longer intact because it used fifty-cent words.

The Merriam-Webster Dictionary defines a fifty-cent word as "an obscure word used to describe a simple idea thus making the user self-important."

There are many problems with MBA-speak introductions:

1. Loss of concentration by the listener
2. The potential for mismatched interpretation
3. Can it be remembered? (I don't think so)
4. The potential for advocacy is lost

That last one is crucial because, as you now know, in order for a person to act on your behalf when you are not present, your brand must be clear as a bell. MBA-speak doesn't lean in that direction.

After working through his stories, the CFO came up with this:

I help companies keep more of the money they earn.

> Keep it simple when introducing yourself.

Better! Going simple, clean, and brief is always a choice. Staying with the smarty pants introduction is a choice, too.

It is straightforward enough that an MBA-speak introduction is too complicated to interpret and remember with all its fifty-cent words. Still, I can't stop there. There are so many stunning examples to share and entertain you with. Here are a few:

- *I help businesses maximize asset values through strategic partnerships and tactical strategies.*

- *I help clients align their strategies, business models, and operating models to achieve competitive advantage and achieve corporate growth, profitability, and performance goals.*

- *I Help Executives Gain Clarity and Move Forward into Radical Fulfillment and Impact. (Excuse the crazy capitalizations; that's another mistake many make.)*

- *Entrepreneurial, analytical, collaborative and innovative Professional Services executive with hands-on large projects experience in Fortune 500 companies across an array of industries.*

- *Creating success thru amplifying impact, forging links others miss, reducing complexity, bridging divides, generating connections, incorporating overlooked voices, communicating data, & increasing accessibility.*

- *History of orchestrating successful changed management in multiple organizations resulting in increased margins, better operations, stronger customer confidence, and improved safety and work environment for its people identify and mitigate risks and drive continuous improvement and efficiency.*

I'll spare you any more of them. The point is, as temping as it is to use MBA-speak—resist. A cleaner, simpler introduction and three or more well-crafted pillars will work harder for you and will be more memorable than the gobbledygook of an MBA-speak introduction.

These examples illustrate that, in addition to the four core problems with MBA-speak mentioned above, another problem surfaces. As these examples show, the more chocked full of multi-syllabic business terms an introduction is, the less likely it will be that the person's profession or industry is evident. The essence of a person's profession is obscured by the noise of the introduction itself.

Ten million plus. As of the writing of this book, that is how many MBAs are represented in LinkedIn in the U.S. Many use MBA-speak in their profiles. Using MBA jargon, including but not limited to the words *disruptive, synergy, conceptualize, disintermediate, globalize, optimization, technology transformation, your guide through uncertainty, blah, blah*... just makes it harder to be remembered and distinguished on LinkedIn. Think "Nike swoosh." Keep it simple when introducing yourself. Leave the MBA-speak for the next time you bump into one of your old professors!

Let's change an MBA-speak introduction into an Art of Hello introduction. Here's one I was sent to critique after a presentation:

I generate millions of dollars as a management and engineering consultant in international manufacturing disputes. (15 words)

You decide if this is better:

I turn manufacturing disputes into profitable outcomes. (7 words)

Skippable Mistake #4: Job Title

One day, I was in my front yard when a neighbor who was having her house painted came over, sharing that she was pleased with the painting company she was using. As a way of offering a referral for the company (acting as an advocate), she said, "Come on over, Paula. I want you to meet the project manager." The man, wearing his classic painter's whites and with brush in hand, introduced himself.

Why am I bringing you a painter's story? Because it made me wonder how many people use the term "project manager" to describe themselves. So, I looked up the job title *Project Manager* on LinkedIn. In the United States, there were about 9,800,000 people using that title that day, and the majority used the title as their headline. The primary title used by nearly ten million people was *the same*: Project Manager.

> The primary title used by nearly ten million people was *the same*: Project Manager.

Project managers (or PMs) are a part of every industry and every profession. It is a generic job title. If you are in IT, finance, marketing, supply chain, compliance, accounting, order processing, or customer service—in virtually every profession, there are PMs that keep the wheels turning. So common is the title, and so widespread its use, that those ten million people on LinkedIn might as well be saying, "I breathe."

We know that the best Art of Hello introduction is the distillation of one's profession. PMs do important work for their organizations. They manage complex processes, keeping small to very large teams working in the same direction. They keep important timelines and deadlines. They manage the scheduling of critical resources. PMs are often assigned to ensure that innovation projects come to completion to meet market deadlines.

Think beyond the title and use an introduction that says more about you

PMs don't show up daily looking for work. Every PM I know hits the ground running every day to keep up with the need for their organizational skills. Poorly organized or sloppy PMs do not keep their jobs. The best PMs are sought-after experts and provide not only organization but, many times, the information for managerial and executive reporting on which business decisions are made.

Yet, as important as the work is, many people who hold that title are willing to come across as generic, if they come across at all. It is counterintuitive. If the work were dull or mundane, sure, hide it with a generic title. But in most cases, it is the opposite.

The basic function of a professional introduction is to represent a person's brand. A well-crafted introduction becomes a brand promise. Remember, *a brand promise is a value or experience that a professional's community can expect to receive every single time they interact with that person.*

If you have a generic job title like PM, staff accountant, operations manager, director, area manager, account executive, product manager, HR business partner, sourcing associate, marketing manager, sales representative, etc., you have a new opportunity. That opportunity is to think beyond the title and use an introduction that says more about you, one that includes your brand promise—the promise you make every day through your work. A more thoughtful introduction will put you (and every one of those nearly ten million people on LinkedIn) on the path to a more descriptive, useful, and memorable introduction.

Here are some ideas for the PM's introduction: *I deliver the promises of the group,* or *Scheduler Extraordinaire!* Or, *Come to me when you need a quick answer on the XYZ project.*

Think about the meaning of the title beyond the fact that it was assigned to you. Consider the brand promise of the job and start thinking about how you would like to be known. Get started on crafting an Art of Hello introduction that will set you apart and provide more information than any generic title ever could.

Let's get back to my neighbor for a moment. Perhaps the painter project manager might introduce himself by saying, *"My job is to make every paint job perfect."* That works!

Skippable Mistake #5: Your Degree Name

Professionals early in their careers are particularly vulnerable to being forgotten when they introduce themselves. They often believe they haven't accumulated enough professional capital to be bold in their self-introductions, they make Mistake #5 in The Art of Hello— they use their degree title as their professional brand.

Leave the degree name in your rearview mirror and craft your own Art of Hello introduction.

You remember Jennifer. She introduced herself with the degree title Water Engineer. Not a completely useless title because it sorts her out from other engineering professionals, but it's far from perfect. With a little inspection, we found that Jennifer was a lot more than a technically trained water engineer. After looking at the impact of Jennifer's work in a larger context, we discovered she was *an economic development professional helping North Texas cities continue to grow for decades to come.*

Like generic job titles, a person is more, and delivers more, than their degree's name describes. Degree titles tend to be generic and mostly the same from college to college. Add more to your introduction; once a person begins to be productive in their career, they have something bigger to say about themselves than merely what degree they earned. Leave the degree name in your rearview mirror and craft your own Art of Hello introduction. Doing so will pay you the dividend of being remembered.

Skippable Mistake #6: Inconsistency

It is well known in the practice of brand building that it's easier for people to remember a brand if it is consistently presented across all channels. It is no different when a person is the brand. The Art of Hello introduction and pillars are the declaration of a person's brand. Of course, no brand is useful without the critical part of "walking the walk" or living the brand promise. It is absolutely a given.

Reinforcement plays an important role in memory formation because it moves the memory from short-term categories to lon-

> Consistently using The Art of Hello introduction helps your network remember you exactly as you want to be remembered.

ger-lasting ones.[19] To establish your professional brand,

19 Ashish Ranpura, "How We Remember, And Why We Forget," *Brain Connection*, March 12, 2013, Retrieved December 22, 2020 from https://brainconnection. brainhq.com/2013/03/12/how-we-remember-and-why-we-forget/.

repetition matters. Two factors are at play: first, the *kind of words used* in The Art of Hello introduction, ones that are simple, clean, unambiguous, and brief; and second, the *places where you use* your introduction.

The powerful action of advocacy—others acting on your behalf when you are not around to represent your-self—is an outcome of The Art of Hello when it's done right. Consistently using The Art of Hello introduction exactly the same way every time helps your network re-member you exactly as you want to be remembered, and it helps them repeat your brand exactly as you would wish. In the ROI section, we looked at all the channels for The Art of Hello introduction: a professional bio, a resume, your company website, LinkedIn and social media profiles, on business cards, in a voicemail greet-ing, in your email signature block, and more. Wherever you are, there your Art of Hello introduction should be. Using specific words consistently throughout your capstone introduction and your pillars multiplies those words through repetition, making a brand memorable and also making it stick.

Every marketer who practices good brand hygiene for their company or product brands will tell you the same thing: Craft your brand carefully, stick to it, and then repeat and proliferate it to your intended audi-ence. It's the same with your professional brand. Craft it carefully, repeat it, and stick with it. The killer of your brand is when you mix it up, using various versions to introduce yourself in person, online, in your resume or bio, and on social media. Be consistent.

The Art of Hello promises that you will be remembered for your unique professional brand. Avoiding the six common mistakes is your head start on getting your brand right and remembered.

The Art of Hello® at a Glance

Chapter Eight

Skippable mistakes – avoid these and you're on your way to getting your Art of Hello right.

- List method
- Chronological
- MBA-speak
- Job title
- Degree name
- Inconsistency

Chapter Nine

Job Seekers, Introverts, and Leaders, Oh My!

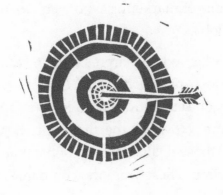

A personal brand, a way to quickly identify and differentiate yourself, is a big arrow in your job-search quiver. Ninety-five percent of recruiters view a competitive personal brand as an essential differentiator for attracting the best applicants in today's workplace, according to a 2015 survey.[20] If you haven't yet crafted an Art of Hello introduction, do so before launching a job search.

---

20 N. Haig, "Your PERSONAL BRAND: Building a professional identity, and promoting it effectively, can be vital to an internal auditor's career," *Internal Auditor*, 75(1) (2018): 57.

> Having an Art of Hello introduction during a job search informs your target market.

It bears repeating that Karen and I met in 2008 when the economy was in freefall. It was a time of massive staff reductions for companies across the country. Karen, like hundreds of thousands of others, was laid off and was going job hunting in a soft economy and a very crowded labor market. There were scores of vice presidents of marketing who were unemployed and looking for jobs.

When we landed on Karen's *biggest, baddest thing* she had ever done—*revitalizing tired brands*—we were able to focus her job search. Karen no longer sought to work just anywhere. Now for the first time, her search was focused on those Dallas-area brands that were tired, past their prime. These were the companies that needed Karen's skills the most; they would value her more, and she could make an impact.

Having an Art of Hello introduction during a job search informs your target market, helping you focus on companies you are best suited for. You can articulate your brand promise and match up with an employer that needs you and your exact experience. There are so many benefits that ride on the back of that short and sweet Art of Hello introduction.

Benefit 1: Having a target market for a job search appropriately narrows the companies you want to contact.

Benefit 2: When you become a candidate at one of the companies in your sights, you will be first among equals. You can articulate your value.

Benefit 3: By having an Art of Hello introduction and well-formed pillars, you can quickly demonstrate competence when asked some form of "Tell me about yourself." You know exactly what you will say. You can deliver two or three of your pillars, and boom, you have successfully and succinctly answered that very hard question. Your competitors for a job, I promise, will either be like the proverbial deer in the headlights or will be droning on and on and on and on until the interviewer is no longer listening.

Not a job seeker today? Okay, this job seeker section might actually be read by a larger audience than just those who are currently looking for work. In the back of your mind, are you thinking about getting a new job? You may be more open to it than you think. Eric Feng, a partner at Kleiner Perkins Caufield & Byers, says, "Only 25% of the workforce is actively looking at any given time, but 85% is willing to talk."[21]

21 C. Ricketts, "The Exact Hiring Formula That Will Help You Find the Right People," *Fast Company*, April 29, 2015, Retrieved on January 28, 2021 from https://www.fastcompany.com/3045448/the-exact-hiring-formula-that-will-help-you-find-the-right-people.

When you are ready, or when an opportunity comes knocking, don't give away a great job prospect because you can't clearly articulate your knowledge or the benefits you bring. A powerful introduction that makes you stand out is the distillation of your professional achievements and credentials. Craft yours and have it ready for the right moment.

A word about LinkedIn and the use of your Art of Hello introduction. There is no better place than LinkedIn to display your Art of Hello introduction. LinkedIn is a professional networking mecca. It's a 24/7 professional billboard for your talents, and it is the epicenter of so much hiring. Place your Art of Hello introduction next to your picture (your professional headshot, not one of you holding a can of beer, wearing a mask, with a poodle, or as a speck on the side of a mountain. Oh, don't get me started!). Go to your profile edit screen and type it in. If you do not do this, LinkedIn will assign you the job title from your most current job and identify you, with your picture, with that title. This is why ten million people in the U.S. are identified as Project Managers. Also, you can include your Art of Hello introduction in the Summary. The Summary section is a couple of thousand characters, so you have plenty of room for your introductions and all the color commentary—your pillars and key search terms—that you would like to display there.

The Use of The Art of Hello for Introverts

I wanted to know what percentage of the population is considered introverted before I wrote this section. It turns out there are a lot of you out there! According to Google search results, as many as 30 to 50 percent of the population identify as introverts. Just a reminder, this isn't the same as being shy. Introverts can be sociable, but they are drained by too much social interaction. Extroverts, of course, are the opposite; social interaction energizes them.

The Art of Hello allows people to create offline, and at their own pace, what they will say about themselves when introduced in social set-

> The Art of Hello branded introduction and its pillars are the perfect tools for introverts.

tings, at business events, or when meeting partners or colleagues for the first time. What a relief! There's a freedom in knowing that you won't have to think on the fly about how to answer the question you know is coming. You'll be ready well in advance for the potentially awkward moment when you must be "on" but don't particularly feel that you are. The Art of Hello is a familiar friend, something known and practiced. It's comfortable and can reduce the anxiety of feeling pushed into social situations that exhaust you.

Add the benefit of comfort to the already robust list of benefits associated with The Art of Hello introduction, and it becomes even more appealing.

Senior Leaders, Professionals and The Art of Hello

> When crafting your Art of Hello introduction, start with the essence of who you are.

For those of us who have worked for a decade or more, an Art of Hello introduction is very useful and easier to devise than it is for a person crafting one early in their career.

Why is an Art of Hello easy to create? First, because there is a richness to a person's career by the second decade of their work life, and beyond. It is a fertile field for describing one's work. Second, there is little or no ambiguity about the personal traits that a person exercises at work by this point in their career. The essence of who they are is very clear. Let's take another look at Mike, the financial advisor we met in Chapter Seven. Mike thought he helped people "over their financial finish lines." Actually, he didn't at all. Instead, Mike helps people become *comfortable and confident in their financial futures*, because that is the essence of who he is.

For senior leaders and professionals, the essence of who we are is already established, and it has been at work for a long time. Maybe you have called it your leadership style. If you vacillate at all in concisely describing your capstone Art of Hello introduction because your delivery is too broad to distill, then you have a wonderful fall back. Describe yourself by using the archetype of the *essence of who you are*. This is clear and well established, and if you look over the arc of your career, it's almost certain you have taken the essence of who you are into every job, every career pivot, and into every interaction with clients and colleagues. When crafting your Art of Hello introduction, start here—with the essence of who you are.

By no means is this the right archetype for every senior professional. Like everyone else, your introduction is your brand promise. In Chapter Ten, a simple three-step process lays out how to arrive at your Art of Hello branded introduction. Follow these steps and see where they lead you.

The Results Are In

As we approach this exact point of peeling back The Art of Hello in many of my presentations, I conduct a poll. Here it is, followed by what it confirms time and time again.

Question 1: Of the people you meet, how many do you think have memorable introductions?

    A. A few

    B. More than 50 percent

    C. 80 percent +

Question 2: Will you work on your Art of Hello introduction and use it?

A. Yes, I want this for myself

B. Maybe, not yet convinced

C. No, it's not for me

Question 3: How many words would you like to use in your Art of Hello introduction?

A. 5-7 words

B. 7-10 words

C. 10+ words

In answering the first question, 90 to 100 percent respond: *A. Very few.*

> Why use ten words if six will do?

In my recruiting practice, I talk with hundreds of people, and very few people are succinct about who they are as professionals. On occasion, one person answers *C. 80 percent +* of people they meet have clear and impactful introductions. When I get that answer, I want to meet that person's friends and colleagues because, as a group, they are extraordinary (though maybe fictitious).

For question two, "Will you work on your Art of Hello introduction and use it?" the answer is almost always unanimous: *Yes, I want this for myself.* Of course, there is always one outlier, a contrarian by nature, who is not convinced that The Art of Hello is for them. That is ok. Variety is the spice of life.

With question three, "How many words would you like to use in your Art of Hello introduction?" the answers are almost always split. An equal number of people select A and B. About ten percent choose C.

You know how I feel about brevity. Remember, Dictionary.com defines brevity as *the quality of expressing much in few words.*

The Art of Hello is a discipline that relies on the fewest words to create the biggest bang while maintaining clarity. So why use ten words if six will do? The goal is to have your advocates recite your Art of Hello introduction exactly, to represent your brand accurately, so that you will be remembered. If you use ten or more words, people will not be able to remember your entire introduction, which will make it impossible for them to repeat it exactly as you intend on your behalf in your absence. The Art of Hello introduction needs to be as short as possible. Always, the fewer words, the better.

Colloquial Sells

It is a thin line that runs between corny and colloquial language in Art of Hello introductions. And how close to the "corny" line a person can get is 100 percent their call. Some people are just more casual and upbeat and prefer less formal language. Perfect is the colloquial option for a person who feels that something catchy and informal suits their brand. Here is the deal—for remembering a person's self-introduction, their brand—colloquial sells.

Appropriately colloquial Art of Hello language is similar to classy language—it is easier to recognize than it is to describe. Colloquial language also tends to create images or pictures with words. The mind's eye is ignited, and, listening to or reading an Art of Hello introduction that uses colorful, colloquial terms offers a bigger overall experience. It has the potential to make the branded introduction even more memorable than a well-crafted, non-colloquial, one.

Here are some examples of introductions that use upbeat, colloquial language.

Hello, I'm Dan Nye, the banking guy! This was the introduction from a man I met at least a year ago. He told me that he has been using this introduction for a decade or more. It's clever. The cadence is catchy, and of course, the refence to Bill Nye, the Science Guy, is fun and unmistakable. I will not forget Dan, especially the next time I am searching for a banker. As Art of Hello introductions go, this one gets two thumbs up.

> Here is the deal for remembering a person's self-introduction. Colloquial sells.

I was presenting The Art of Hello to a Fujitsu leadership class, and during the workshop hour, I met Ron and his colleague, who were working on their Art of Hello introductions. The core of Ron's job is preventative maintenance. His friend came up with this for Ron: *I'm Ron, and I put the 24/7 in the 365.* I get this! Ron is relied upon to keep systems going on a 24-hour, 7-days a week, 365-days a year basis. It fits the brand promise that Ron makes. So simple, and fun. If it suits Ron to use it, it's a wonderful introduction. He can easily follow up with a pillar that adds depth.

There are other colloquial introductions whose values are in the eye of the teller. I find that they miss the mark, leaning toward corny, too casual, or slightly confusing. But you decide.

- *I perform organizational origami by adding a dimension to anything falling flat.* I get the contrast between 3D origami and something that is flat. But the mental picture of folding paper into birds missed the mark for me. I find myself with that *"what?"* head tilt when hearing it.

- *Just a girl trying to find her way in this world.* From LinkedIn. Great opening line for a sitcom, but for a professional, I think it's ditsy.

- *Anything you can do we can do better together.* A man named Mitchell offered this to me after an Art of Hello presentation. Although heading in the right direction, this one is vague; it could be used by anyone at all. It's generic. The brand promise is there, but I don't get a clue about the person's profession or industry.

- *Think of me as the modern-day Scooby-Doo; here to solve and optimize your solutions (minus the monsters, of course)*. From LinkedIn. This one walks very close to crossing the corny line. I get the Scooby-Doo reference and the monsters, but I still have to ask, is this professional enough? If this person is a flexible, gets-things-done pro, then maybe an upgrade from a cartoon character is best.

- Manufacturing and selling private label and branded men's underwear, this executive feels comfortable with this colloquial gem: *I cover the asses of the masses.* (Don't you know this man is a lot of fun!)

The Responsibility of the Listener in an Exchange

A note about the responsibility of the listener in remembering your introduction. Up to this point, we've put the responsibility of being remembered solely on the speaker. That's you or me when introducing ourselves. It is incumbent upon me to deliver an Art of Hello introduction and pillars that are concise and memorable. But there are two parties involved in this exchange. One is the listener, who to this point is not on the hook at all. I looked into the listener's responsibility for remembering me, and it brought me full circle. Generally, the listener will retain information, in this case about you or me, when they are interested in the subject matter.

The key to a good memory is your level of interest. The more interest you show in a topic, the more likely it will imprint itself on your brain.[22]

Ah ha! The listener has to be interested to imprint the memory. So, you and I have to make it interesting! In tennis, I guess we would say that the ball is still in our court.

Champions keep playing until they get it right.
–Billie Jean King

And so, when you put the twin forces of information overload and decision fatigue together with the reality that our brains are not meant to handle this much information, that's where you really find the importance of building a personal brand and a strong one. When you build a strong personal brand, you are essentially elevating your reputation and the recognition of your value in the market so that people don't have to decide about you—they already know.

So, I'll say this again because it is an important point: When people are making tens of thousands of micro-decisions on a daily basis—and you divide that by the fact that our brains are not meant to operate in this climate of exponential information—it's really important to be known as a sure thing. Right? You need to be a person that people don't have to decide about because they

---

22 Kansas State University, "What's your name again? Lack of interest, not brain's ability, may be why we forget," *ScienceDaily*, June 20, 2012, Retrieved November 5, 2020 from www.sciencedaily.com/releases/2012/06/120620113027.html.

already know your brand. Don't contribute to decision fatigue. If you build a powerful personal brand, chances are good your ideas will be heard, respected, and acted upon. You've made yourself easy to remember.

The Art of Hello® at a Glance
Chapter Nine

- For job seekers, The Art of Hello:
  - o Focuses your target
  - o Makes you first among equals with the competition
  - o Helps articulate your value
  - o Quickly demonstrates competence when asked some form of "tell me about yourself"
- For Introverts, The Art of Hello:
  - o Is a familiar friend, something known and well-practiced
  - o Is comfortable and can reduce anxiety
- For senior leaders and professionals, The Art of Hello:
  - o Synthesizes the richness of your career

- Use colloquial language for your Art of Hello:
  - o If something catchy and informal suits your brand
  - o If you want a surefire way of being remembered—when it comes to a person's self-introduction, colloquial sells if they can sell it

Chapter Ten

Three Steps to Creating an Art of Hello® Introduction of Your Own, Now

Your Art of Hello introduction is a reusable career asset. It sets you apart from others in your profession. It demonstrates your executive presence, establishes you as consciously competent, creates a memorable brand statement, and forms the basis for building advocates for your career. WOW. That is a lot of benefit on the back of one hour and a few words!

Step One: Distill Your Professional Brand

Distilling your professional deliverables, clearly articulating your brand promise, and then codifying it into your Art of Hello introduction is a fine career accomplishment. It may not be easy, but it costs only an hour of your time, and you will have a huge return on that one-hour investment.

- **Hear yourself and know yourself**

Before you can begin however, you must know yourself. The purpose of the first step is to examine your professional outcomes in order to identify the daily patterns that represent your brand promise. Many of us run from one task to the next. We keep busy with wave after wave of work, rarely stopping to assess, write down, or discuss the successes of the day. Few professions have a final definition of success. In sales or transactional professions, a successful outcome is clear when sales are made, the deal is done, and the ink is dry. However, too often, many of us don't have an exclamation point at the end of our work to help us define success.

Defining your deliverables, your brand promise, and successes—which are the hallmark of your work—is done through storytelling. These little and big successes, the points of pride, illuminate the brand promise you make and are the basis of your Art of Hello introduction. In Step One, the goal is to find the pattern of your successful work.

- **Partner up and tell stories**

This is where working with a partner is useful. Find someone who will be impartial, listening to your stories and reflecting back to you what they hear. Remember Mike? When I met him, he promised to "put people over their financial finish lines." I sat quietly (acting as the partner in this exercise) and asked him to tell me stories of six clients who liked his work well enough to refer him to other potential clients. You may recall Mike told me six stories, and I took careful notes. At the end of all six, I reported what I had heard. Mike actually put zero of the clients "over their financial finish lines." Instead, he listened to them, and over time, he helped them solve financials problems, making them more *comfortable and confident in their financial futures.*

Before going through that exercise, Mike hadn't seen the pattern in the work he did with his clients. He also did not recognize the value of his brand's authenticity. Mike had been introducing himself with a spiffy, yet inaccurate, tagline. Prior to this conversation with me as Mike's listening partner, he had viewed each client as unique (and they are), yet he failed to see whether his own brand delivery worked for the whole set. Taken together, his clients formed a continuum of his work outcomes. All of Mikes clients succeeded, but no one retired early or got rich. No finish line was breached. Each client was still a work in progress, but now, with Mike's help, they were more *comfortable and confident in their financial futures.* It took telling the six stories, my willingness to listen hard, and Mike's courage to hear my summary for him to see the pattern. Mike had no idea that he wasn't being authentic when he used the jazzy tagline. By hearing my summary, that his clients were getting something highly valuable from him along with his technical advice, Mike took away a fresh, authentic Art of Hello introduction that day.

> Defining your deliverables, your brand promise, and successes is done through storytelling.

Using a partner allows a non-biased listener to "hear between the lines" and identify patterns. Most of us are too close to our daily work to see the forest for the trees. This is the benefit of adding a partner to the mix.

Remember, both the storyteller and the listener-partner have to be able to look for the overall theme of the stories, get out of the weeds, and see the recurring patterns. This will be harder if the two paired up are both from professions where details are the lifeblood of good work. Two engineers, accountants, or software developers working together may be hard pressed to focus on the patterns and see the big picture of the brand promises, tucked into the success stories. Mix it up, put a generalist with a technician when pairing up. You both will have a better outcome.

To make this exercise successful, be sure you allow yourself and your listener-partner to generalize the impact of your work and stories, to look for the arch that best describes your professional deliverables. These stories can revolve around your credentials as well as your success stories. They can be the work you produce, or perhaps the way your work differentiates you.

As an example, I have worked with an administrative assistant named Ellen at three companies over many years. She followed me to companies as I changed jobs. We have a good partnership between us. Ellen is highly productive; she accomplishes a lot, and she is organized and disciplined. As important as she is to administrative work—keeping me on my path, sorting out the details—she also fills the important role as the emotional glue for our work groups and departments. Ellen is foremost a people person. Her upbeat, happy, playful attitude, and her ability to know team members' strengths and even their moods, allows her to navigate the people dynamics of the groups, relieving stress and bringing a little sunshine to the office every day. (We had a laugh when we saw that she had placed binoculars on the office window ledge overlooking a hotel pool. Sure enough, on occasion, one of us would amazingly catch a skinny dipper!)

When Ellen tells her stories, they not only focus on the deliverables of daily administrative work but also on the joy of remembering birthdays, bringing cakes, and celebrating the wins of the team. These activities are front and center in her overall impact and effectiveness at doing her job. Like Mike, the financial advisor, Ellen's archetype is the *essence of who she is*. It differentiates her from others in her profession.

- **360-degree success stories**

A second method for drawing out the information to craft your Art of Hello introduction is examining a 360-degree success story. Recall for yourself and your listening partner a big or important project that you successfully completed. None of us works in a vacuum, and we acknowledge that big projects are completed by teams. Still, there is probably something that was assigned that you contributed to in a key way, so concentrate on that. From what you know that was actually said about your work on the project (or what you believe honestly would be said about your contribution), "interview" the parties connected to the project, and ask them for comments about your work.

> How your work is seen is your current brand promise in action.

Gathering information from a 360-degree review means hearing from:

- your boss
- your coworkers
- the people who report to you
- your internal or external clients
- the business partners on your projects
- others who may have seen you in action

All of these parties experience your work from a slightly different vantage point. With the collection of these data points, you can sew together a pattern of how people see you. How your work is seen is your current brand promise in action. Now you have the basis for articulating your brand and arriving at The Art of Hello distillation you seek.

- **Use your old 30-second drill**

Another way to hear yourself and know yourself is by looking back at your old 30-second drill. You may be surprised to hear me say this, but dust it off and use it to help you craft your new introduction. Take the message you captured in that speech and use it as the basis for your Art of Hello introduction and pillars. Try to see through the many words to the overall message and edit it down to its core. Shape it up into the magic six to ten words that will give you an impactful and memorable Art of Hello introduction. This is certainly easier said than done, but it is possible. It's a shortcut that can replace the route of telling all your success stories to a listening partner. It's worth a try. If it doesn't work, go the storytelling or points-of-pride route.

In the event that the distillation of your 30-second drill does not net you a great Art of Hello introduction, it still may be useful as a repository for some of your pillars. The 30-second drill likely has your success stories tucked into it. It may contain the best of your industry jargon, or it might include some quantitative results that you are still proud of and that represent your brand. These are the makings of the pillars you want to have ready at a moment's notice to support and fill out the brand promise of your Art of Hello introduction. Lift these from the 30-second drill and polish them up as a pillar. No use reinventing the wheel. If you already have the 30-second drill collateral, don't throw it away; look for its re-use potential. Dissect it and use it differently. Fair enough.

- **The long form**

Storytelling with a partner can be just plain uncomfortable for some. Some people want an Art of Hello introduction but still have the "it's bragging" ghost hanging over them. Some are simply introverts and telling their success stories does not come naturally—the effort can be exhausting.

Similarly, there are detail-oriented people whose point-of-pride success stories tend to be long and laden with the specifics. If this is you, don't fight it; it's your nature. Just find another way to work through the background revelations to uncover the little jewel that is The Art of Hello introduction. Don't let the discomfort of storytelling be the reason you abandon the effort.

My friend Ginny Gray and I met for breakfast one day with the goal of crafting her Art of Hello introduction. Ginny and I had worked together on a project and became friends, so we had a high level of comfort with one another. We both went into the morning expecting we could nail it and land on a great Art of Hello introduction for her.

Then it got complicated. Ginny is a Ph.D., a corporate executive with responsibilities at the C-suite and board level of a Fortune 500 company, and she has been a consultant to the stars in her profession. Ginny's success stories were many, and she saw each of her numerous roles and positions as unique from one another, not as part of a single continuum. Our eggs were getting cold, and we were not getting closer to synthesizing her career into anything close to an Art of Hello capstone. When the meal was over, and we had our fill of coffee, we agreed to call it a day. Ginny chose to go home and sit at her desk to write out her point-of-pride success stories and then send them to me. And she did.

A week or so later, I opened a five-page, single-spaced Word document from Ginny. Being one who always overachieves, she had. Truth was, I was reluctant to read the whole document, as I was that day—like most—pressed for time. I slid my curser down the densely written pages to the end. And what to my wondering eyes should appear, but four bullets summarizing Ginny's professional accomplishments and the solid basis for the distillation of her professional brand for her Art of Hello introduction.

I call this the *long form*. If you are a person who craves more data, or you always want to cover topics chronologically, or you just prefer

> Don't let the discomfort of storytelling be the reason you abandon your Art of Hello introduction.

working alone, then the long form is the perfect method for you to arrive at your Art of Hello *"AH-HA!"* moment. Sit yourself down at your computer and go for it. Then, if a partner is helpful, partner up. As it was with Ginny, she sorted it out on her own. She did not need me. Ginny saw the forest for the trees, it just took her a few thousand words to get there. No harm, no foul. We all process and express our thoughts differently, and The Art of Hello creation process is adaptable.

When you finish Step One toward having an Art of Hello introduction of your own, using the "know yourself" techniques that suit you best, go ahead and check to see which archetype your introduction falls into. Chances are pretty good that your Art of Hello introduction will fit into one of them. I don't think I've ever worked with a person whose Art of Hello introduction didn't. Do not start with archetypes and work backward to your own, do the work to craft your Art of Hello introduction and see where your introduction lands.

1. *The Biggest, Baddest Thing I Have Done*
   Karen: *I revitalize tired brands.*

2. *My Newest Accomplishment*
   Shaunna: *I help manufacturing plants become LEED certified.*

3. *My Work in a Bigger Context*
   Jennifer: *I am an economic development professional; I keep North Texans in water for decades to come.*

4. *The Results of What I Do*
   John: *I am a billion-dollar brand builder on the back of old-fashioned brick and mortar retail.*

5. *The Essence of Who I Am*
   Mike: *I help my clients become comfortable and confident in their financial futures.*

6. *My Repeated Successes*
   Bill: *Introducing the right people, for the right reasons, at the right time.*

7. *My Aspirations*
   Christina: *By day, I sell cloud technology; by heart, I advocate for organ donations.*

Step Two: Build Your Pillars

The Art of Hello introduction you craft is your durable brand promise. It is the capstone statement and the jumping off point to fill out your story. It is a springboard to conversations that matter.

Pillars support and fill out your professional brand. (Chapter Four describes pillars and their attributes.) The second step in completing The Art of Hello brand introduction is to craft your pillars. Pillars are the way you provide people the fullness of your professional story. I recommend that people craft three to eight pillars. These include your credentials, skills, experiences, capabilities, and notable successes. They can be targeted to the audience or person you are talking to and used when needed to complete your professional story.

Pillars also have the wonderful property of adapt-ability—they can be crafted as answers to questions yet to be asked. If your Art of Hello is at all intriguing and done right, then you can anticipate the natural questions to follow. Preparing a pillar or two is a great way to prepare for the question you know is coming, and you'll have the right answer on the tip of your tongue.

Remember, your pillars should:

1. Highlight the important aspects of your professional achievements. Pillars can spotlight an advanced degree or professional credentials, for example. A pillar can be the special work you did on a start-up or product launch. Bring in the stories that put a smile on your face.

2. Focus on your points of pride. Bring out the work you have done that sets you apart and constitutes the *biggest, baddest things* you have done, or that shines a light on your best professional qualities.

3. Answer common questions or objections. Pillars are the perfect tool to craft the answer to an objection or concern that you anticipate, or to get a jump on a question that often comes up when talking about your career. You will know in advance the right answer and can deliver it perfectly without any awkwardness.

4. Provide the best place for use of industry or professional jargon. Use jargon in a pillar, *not* in your Art of Hello introduction. Judicious use of jargon comes with real benefits. One is tribal identification. When used carefully, jargon quickly connects a person to a group or profession. It can connote authority or mastery of a field. Jargon can help cut through long explanations and create brief pillars.

5. Be scripted and memorized. The most natural conversations are spontaneous, and you get that impact with your Art of Hello introduction and pillars when they are delivered exactly the same way every time. Do they lose their freshness? No, they don't. The paradox is that the better scripted and rehearsed your Art of Hello introduction and pillars are, the more natural they sound when spoken. Memorizing them allows them to slip off your tongue with a natural and perfect delivery.

6. Work as internal organization introductions. Your Art of Hello capstone statement might sound a little "off" to people inside your company who, even if they have not met you before, have more context about what you do than someone outside your organization.

7. Provide a place where numbers shine. The sales and production increases, the time and money saved, and the customers added belong in the perfectly crafted pillar. These are very descriptive of your value.

Including the numbers adds the proof that you deliver on your brand promise.

8. Follow the simple, clear, authentic, and rather brief rules of The Art of Hello introduction. Sure, you have more than six to ten words to spend on any pillar, but you still want to craft them tightly. They'll be easier to say and easier to remember.

Step Three: Test Your Art of Hello Introduction

- **The gut check**

Your Art of Hello introduction has to feel right to you. Like shopping for sneakers, this is an exercise of comfort. The comfort we seek here is the absolute feeling that you will be comfortable time and again letting your Art of Hello introduction represent you professionally. If you find yourself doubting the introduction or wiggling in your chair when you read or hear it, then it's not right for you. This is a test of authenticity.

> No matter how good The Art of Hello phrase sounds, if it is not right for you, it's not right.

Remember Shaunna from Chapter Three? When she and I reconvened to update her Art of Hello introduction, Shaunna said, "When I land on my Art of Hello introduction, I will know it. I will have no doubt; it will feel right."

This is an important gut test. No matter how good The Art of Hello phrase sounds, if it is not right for you, it's not right. Remember Mike who helped his clients get over their financial finish lines? Except, he didn't. A rinse and repeat were necessary for Mike. He had to give his brand a second look, and you can too. Even if you spent the time and made a gallant try, it has to feel right to be right.

- **The CASBAH test**

I put the core tenets of The Art of Hello into an acronym program online and a list was presented. From that list, I chose CASBAH.

The CASBAH test asks this question. Is The Art of Hello introduction you created clear, actual, specific, brief, authentic, and honest?

Clear	Brief
Well-defined	Short
Sharp	Concise
Distinct	Succinct
Clear-cut	To-the-point
Unclouded	Terse

Actual	Authentic
Real	True
Definite	Reliable
Genuine	Dependable
Concrete	Trustworthy
Tangible	Realistic

Specific	Honest
Exact	Truthful
Precise	Frank
Detailed	Candid
Unambiguous	Straightforward

The primary emphasis of the CASBAH test is authenticity and brevity. Being authentic and honest are the bedrock of The Art of Hello introduction. Self-analysis is necessary to examine authenticity. If an introduction sounds spiffy and you like the marketing appeal, but the authentic DNA is not there, then it's not good enough. Go for the real deal. Bring Mike to mind. Remember, there were no financial finish lines in sight, and I found him out in a ten-minute conversation. Mike didn't intend to deceive, he just fell into the trap of a marketing tagline, rather than finding the authentic distillation of his professional deliverables.

Once authenticity and brevity are confirmed, test for clarity. The ruination of clarity is most likely the attractive lure of MBA-speak. We looked at scads of fancy-pants examples in Chapter Eight, and as we saw so many times, the more multi-syllabic words there are and the more sophisticated the terms, the more puzzling the underlying message of the introduction. As great as all the industry terms and modern business language is, if the listener can't "get it" the second it's said or read, then the hard-working aspect of The Art of Hello introduction is lost. If the listener has to parse out meaning from the terms or sentence, they stop listening and *maybe* start on the mental process necessary to understand your message. The fleeting opportunity to be remembered is gone. MBA-speak is alluring but beware of its appeal and resist the MBA word selection in favor of a simpler, clearer word choice.

Jargon fits into this category, requiring you to test for clarity. As described in Chapter Four, judicious use of industry jargon provides the wonderful benefits of identifying you as part of a profession or tribe. Additional benefits include connoting authority and using it as a tool for brevity. But your Art of Hello introduction goes off track if you use too much jargon. If the terms you use give the listener the impression that the introduction, and therefore the introducer, is pompous, then the jargon has gone too far and should be pulled back in favor of more common language.

> Generic titles need to be replaced with more personally specific word choices.

By narrowing your aperture and using words that describe you specifically, your brand promise can differentiate you from the general population. Introductions that make claims including *hard working, strategic, team player, detail-oriented,* and so forth, lose their effectiveness. Few, if any of us, will admit to not being a hard-working team player. The paradox is that simple and clear words or terms such as these are so generic that they mean *everyone*, and the impact of your unique introduction is lost.

Lack of specificity can be the curse of generic titles like PM, sales executive, staff accountant, superintendent, and many more that are common in every industry. By this point in studying The Art of Hello, we know that generic titles need to be replaced with more personally specific word choices. The shame is that they are hard to give up. My advice: force yourself.

A quick online search reveals that there are 171,000 words in the English language. Of those, 20,000 to 30,000 are frequently used. With all those words available, there have to be some special ones that describe you.

Do not move forward in using an introduction that is not good enough. The phrase "Good enough is good enough" does not apply here. The Art of Hello introduction and its pals, the pillars, represent your professional brand, your hard work, your dedication, your integrity. There is no room for "just ok" when it comes to your Art of Hello introduction. Perfect is the goal, every time.

- **Phone a friend**

Once you've passed the CASBAH test, then phone a friend—or two or three. Call an old colleague, current colleague, past boss, or advisor and let them know that you are crafting your brand introduction, and you want their opinion as to whether it represents you well. You want to get their first reaction. Hopefully it will be, "That is exactly you." If you get that reaction, you likely have a home run. But if you do not, it isn't the end of the road for the introduction you were feeling good about and that passed the CASBAH test.

Phone a friend is just one of three important tests, and it does not stand alone as a deal killer. When you call on a friend or colleague and elicit their help, they likely want to

> Your best Art of Hello introduction is how you want to be known *now*.

actually help. Maybe they think it's wimpy to just agree with you and your brand statement. Maybe they think that unless they make a suggestion or contribution, they haven't fulfilled your request for help. So, a word of caution, *Phone a friend* is useful, but it is not the end-all, be-all in judging your introduction.

You'll want to get one more piece of information from your friend. Ask if they can repeat your introduction back to you. Hearing your Art of Hello introduction just once may or may not be enough for them to gain instant recall, but you'll find out if they get close. Ideally, along with them saying, "Yes, it's you," they can also remember and repeat your introduction right back to you. This is a high bar. The reality is that you will be using your Art of Hello in all communications channels and using it over a period of time. Repetition will make remembering it easier. Repetition of your Art of Hello introduction is like hearing a song over again. Each time you hear it, it becomes more memorable.

Hopefully, this book has provided you with the tools to craft your unique Art of Hello introduction. In keeping with the ultimate trifecta, here is a simple, clear, and brief summary of this book's most important takeaways.

1. Avoid the "so what?" reaction triggered by the list method
2. Distill your experience, don't recite everything you have ever done
3. Use pillars as your jumping off point
4. How to use pillars
5. One hour for your best ROI
6. Avoidable Mistakes

- **An example of The Art of Hello, tested**

You remember Shaunna, who I introduced in Chapter Three. She *helped manufacturing plants become LEED certified*. But a decade later Shaunna, had grown out of that introduction. A fresh look at her brand resulted in Shaunna 2.0: *Growing executive capabilities with head and heart*. Arriving at that contemporary brand introduction required a lot of work from Shaunna and me. We created many Art of Hello introductions that were close to describing the essence of Shaunna's current consulting practice. Here they are:

- *Executive consultation through leadership of the heart*
- *Executive consultant, where doing well is judged by doing good*

- *Executive consultation, where results intersect with compassion*
- *Headstrong consultation, heartfelt results*
- *Stretching executive capabilities, from the head and heart*
- *Serious business consulting delivered from the heart*
- *Compassionate consulting, the people side of profits*
- *I help executives balance profits and people*
- *I help executives grow people and profits*

All of these Art of Hello introductions are close to her brand promise. They all passed the gut check test. We applied the CASBAH test, again, all of them passed. It wasn't until Shaunna tested them with "Phone a friend" that the real and best Art of Hello introduction surfaced. Earlier, we discussed the benefits of advocates and fans, and this is where your advocates can really make a difference. People who care about you professionally will give you careful counsel. For Shaunna, *"Growing executive capabilities with head and heart"* is the essence of who she is. And yes, when Shaunna's profession evolved, so did her Art of Hello introduction. It is worth noting that Shaunna's archetype changed from her *newest accomplishment* to *the essence of who she is*. It's always been the case: your best Art of Hello introduction is how you want to be known *now*.

The Art of Hello® at a Glance

Chapter Ten

- Three steps to creating an Art of Hello introduction of your own

  o Step 1: Summarize - Hear Yourself and Know Yourself

  o Step 2: Build Your Pillars

  o Step 3: Test Your Art of Hello Introduction

    - Gut check

    - CASBAH

    - Phone a friend

Chapter Eleven

A Story Is Worth a Thousand Words

The goal of this book is to provide you with the tools to craft a unique Art of Hello introduction that will serve your career well and ensure that you are remembered for your professional accomplishments.

Unlearn the obsolete elevator speech and the dated 30-second drill and replace them with the updated Art of Hello branded introduction and its useful pillars. It will pay off in huge dividends. But you don't have to take my word for it. Here are more testimonials from people I have met on The Art of Hello journey.

Success Stories Using The Art of Hello Introduction

— **Susan Staub**

Soon after speaking at a conference, I received the following note.

Paula, I took your advice at the IABC Conference and introduced myself to someone: "Hi, I'm Susan Staub. I build and fix internal communications." Not only did the person love the statement, but someone from another part of the room chased me down and said, "I hear you build and fix internal communications. We need to talk."

Thank you!

Lesson: Less is more.

— **Peggy Ethridge**

Recently, I received this email from my friend Peggy.

Paula, I wanted to tell you this experience I had. I was at a luncheon of women where everyone went around the table and introduced themselves and what they did. When it was my turn, I just said, "I work with professionals and their families to help them become work optional." I actually got applause! Everyone then exclaimed that this was a great introduction. I owe this to you, and thanks!

Lesson: Start working on your Art of Hello introduction today and wait for the applause!

— **Adrienne Ciletti**

Just days after Adrienne was in the audience for an Art of Hello presentation, I received this note.

Had to text you to tell you I used my new brand to introduce myself at a career fair yesterday and it worked so well I now say that "I am a communications professional with a passion for employee engagement and storytelling." I got raised eyebrows, smiles, and even an "Oh, that's good." I had their attention when I told them about my background and what I was looking for.

Lesson: The right introduction can get you the right attention.

— **Cindy Anderson**

After having a phone conversation about The Art of Hello with my longtime friend Cindy, she had a chance to use her Art of Hello introduction, and good things happened. Here is her testimonial.

Hi Paula, I want to update you on my Art of Hello. I did my homework, and I practiced my introduction. I landed on, "Hello I'm Cindy, a recruiter. I simplify the hiring process." I then used my new introduction at a systems user group meeting. It worked well as I am working with two new candidates who were in attendance. In addition, a manager that I have known is getting approval to work with me to fill her open sales positions.

I also used my new intro with another prospective client and received (this week) a job order to fill an accountant position. My manager is loving it!

Lesson: Nothing beats clear, simple, and brief for getting the introduction response you deserve.

— **Mitra**

Meet Mitra, an accomplished and tenured senior IT Developer. Like others in her field, she introduced herself with a string of acronyms and alphabet soup, and a list of the many applications she had developed and the platforms she had worked with. After seeing The Art of Hello presentation, Mitra introduced herself to me in this way. *"I love to make computers run faster."* WOW! I know her profession, her passion, and her personality through these seven words. I call that elegant code.

Lesson: Technical jargon may not enrich the opportunity to distinguish yourself. Go simple and back it up with more detailed pillars.

— **McKee Stewart**

McKee was online when I presented The Art of Hello via Zoom. We didn't meet then, but a few days later, I received this email from him.

I attended "The Art of Hello" presentation you made on August 17th. I found it very helpful in developing my brand statement for my current job search: "I help companies find money with projects, processes, and people." I haven't landed yet, but it generates a lot of follow up questions where I can provide examples and starts interesting conversations.

Lesson: Increase engagement through simplicity and clarity.

— Jennifer Carter

Jennifer is a career consultant. After learning the concepts of The Art of Hello, Jennifer landed on this self-introduction. *"Elevating the careers of ambitious women."* It is the essence of Jennifer's profession, and it is clear, short, and distinctive. The best part is that Jennifer reports that when she changed from her old self-introduction (which started with her marketing background and wound around to her consulting practice), to her new Art of Hello introduction, it immediately caused her LinkedIn network requests to increase by 30 percent—and she has sustained it.

Lesson: Having a crystal clear and appealing Art of Hello brand statement has many benefits, growing your valued LinkedIn network is just one of them. Congrats, Jennifer.

The Art of Hello® at a Glance

Chapter Eleven

- The Art of Hello introductions work
- They fulfill the promise of being remembered
- These introductions have many benefits
- They're free

In Closing...

No matter what your profession, The Art of Hello keystones of simplicity, clarity, and brevity apply. I'll leave you with a perfect example from a cultural touchstone of a simple introduction that was used to great effect...

"This here is Miss Bonnie Parker.
I'm Clyde Barrow. **We rob banks.***"*

Appendix A:

The Art of Hello® Examples from Many Professions

Many of the people whose Art of Hello introductions are listed below are friends and colleagues. A few of the examples used are of people I found on LinkedIn and haven't had the pleasure of meeting. I've divided them by profession. All are great examples of perfect Art of Hello introductions. Enjoy.

Financial Planners/Wealth Manager

- *I help people become comfortable and confident in their financial futures.*
- *I help turn current wealth into generational wealth.*
- *I work with select families to make work optional.*
- *Helping clients to use their money to have the lives they want.*

Internal Auditor

- *I help Bank of America become a better version of itself.*

Controller/Accountant

- *Every CFO needs a great Controller. I'm that guy.*
- *I help companies keep more of the money they earn.*
- *By the numbers, I help companies accelerate growth.*
- *I drive revenue growth in startups.*
- *Decision support through precise accounting practices.*
- *Accounting executive, helping companies avoid risk.*
- *From accounting to insurance, I do the numbers.*
- *Accounting wizard. No magic, just precision.*
- *Using accounting, I break out of the typical 9-5 to beat the competition.*
- *Refining the way we do business every day.*
- *Providing the right information to the right people at the right time.*
- *CFO. Financially minded, process driven.*
- *High profits through high touch financial communication.*

IT/Process

- *Helping businesses succeed with new technologies.*
- *Helping companies harden their data security.*
- *I find innovative ways to streamline processes.*
- *I transform data centers from dated to innovative.*

Sports Careers

- *As past NHL, I bring professional league CFO skills to my clients.*

- *All around marketer, I am the hybrid club in your golf bag.*
- *Making NFL images a part of every American's life.*

Past Military

- *A leader in business and battle.*

Non-Profit/Civic

- *I connect forward thinking people with innovative opportunities.*
- *I help people make better lives by giving back to the community.*
- *Striving to elevate society one contribution at a time, for life.*
- *Empowering Central Texans to transform their lives through work!*

Career Coach

- *Helping organizations build leaders and leaders build careers.*
- *Elevating the careers of ambitious women.*
- *Advisor, helping people move their big ideas forward.*

Marketing

- *I revitalize tired brands.*
- *Connecting the dots that turn shoppers into buyers.*
- *My passion is to make online experiences memorable.*
- *Making ginger ale cool!*

- *I help small brands tell big stories.*
- *I help businesses become memorable.*
- *I ignite brands and fans.*
- *Building communities around brands people love.*
- *I build brands that do good.*
- *I cure CMO headaches.*
- *I deliver brand personalization.*
- *I help businesses find truth hidden in data.*

Real Estate

- *I help people start young, live well. I'm your realtor for life.* (residential)
- *Simply solving complex real estate issues.* (commercial)

Sales

- *I can make your business goals a reality.*
- *Delivering more than owners think they can afford.*
- *Linking arms with partners to grow revenue.*

Corporate Education

- *I make companies Harvard smart.*

Recruiter

- *I fill hard to fill positions.*
- *I make hiring easy.*
- *Connecting great people with great companies.*

Airline Industry Software

- *I help airlines to fly on time.*

Physician and Medical Researcher

- *I build medical programs that increase the health of communities.*

Nutritionist

- *Changing kids' lives one plate at a time.*

Municipal Government Finance

- *Making the needs and the money match.*

Retail Executive

- *I reinvent retail to wow customers like you.*

Electrical Engineer

- *I design circuits that work.*

Artist

- *Artist, reducing landfill waste.*

Construction

- *I don't just build...I build relationships.*
- *I build communities by building Kroger stores.*

Resume Writer

- *Ready to empower job seekers.*

Corporate Trainer

- *Growth to ensure the future success of the organization.*

Aerospace

- *I create strategies in aerospace to make the future approachable.*

Consultant

- *I will help lead your company to success, while helping the community prosper.*

Health and Wellness Advocate

- *Hope dealer.*

Appendix B:

The Art of Hello® "CliffsNotes Style"

Chapter One

- This book is written for all professionals who care about their careers, their businesses, and their professional brands. The Art of Hello is a fresh approach to being remembered. Useful to professionals from the start of their careers through senior executives with decades of professional accomplishments, The Art of Hello replaces the old-fashioned elevator speech and debunks the 30-second drill. Crafting an Art of Hello branded introduction is a must. It's a career asset that you cannot afford to be without.

- Talking too much when introducing yourself can set off the *"So what"* trigger.

- The elevator speech and the 30-second drill make you forgettable. A better choice is a succinct brand label for yourself.

- People who know your brand can act as a large sales-force for advancing your career.
- With a memorable brand introduction, your network can recite your brand exactly and pass it on easily.
- Your brand should have no ambiguity about it. It's absolutely clear, simple, and truthful.
- Being remembered or not being remembered are your only choices.
- Daily information floods us from a zillion social media outlets, we learn to tune it out, and that is one of the drawbacks of elevator speeches—people have become pros at tuning them out.
- Problems with the elevator speech or 30-second drill: they are simply too self-centered, and they are not memorable because of the level of detail. Memorized and uselessly long, boring monologues about oneself are easily and immediately forgotten. Using an elevator speech can make you look like you can't *net-it-out*.

Chapter Two

- The Art of Hello is the distillation of your professional life, not a list of everything you've ever done.
- The elevator speech and its friend the 30-second drill are dead. Long live The Art of Hello.

- As professionals, we all deserve to be known for our achievements and to be understood for our value proposition.

- With a clear and concise statement, you make the most of each introduction, both in person and online.

- Clarity is King.

- Until now we haven't been shown how to be remembered in a noisy world.

- High stakes outcome—be remembered or forgotten. It is in your hands.

Chapter Three

- Either we are remembered, or we are forgotten. There's not a lot of middle ground.

- The majority of professionals struggling to describe themselves are babbling along and being forgotten even as they speak.

- Many people in the same profession list their tactical work and are thus indistinguishable from one another through their introductions.

- The *list* method of introduction is a poor means of being remembered, yet it's still pervasive in every profession and industry.

- List-making is a substitute for a real introduction. People speak in lists because, until now, no one has provided a better way for them to introduce themselves.

- Archetypes are formats to which The Art of Hello introductions adhere.

  The first two archetypes are:

  o *The Biggest, Baddest Thing I Have Done*
  o *My Newest Accomplishment*

- Effective Art of Hello Introduction Rules

  Your personal Art of Hello introduction must be—

  o Meaningful
  o Authentic
  o Unambiguous
  o Differentiating
  o Brief
  o Clear and simple

- Reasons for crafting an Art of Hello for yourself

  o Just by having a well-conceived Art of Hello introduction, you separate yourself from the pack.
  o No two people have the same experiences. Even if each of you are in the same profession, your brand statement is unique to your experience.
  o Done right, your Art of Hello introduction is your brand promise.
  o The ability to be remembered is a valuable arrow in your professional quiver.

o People who know your brand become your advocates and fans, and they can act on your behalf when you aren't present to represent yourself.

o You control your own brand and your brand promise.

o Only brevity can make it memorable.

o The Art of Hello is important for job seekers; it informs and focuses your job search.

o It answers that awful, but often asked question, "Tell me about yourself."

o Will allow you to stand out in a crowd.

Chapter Four

• The Art of Hello introductions are the jumping off point, pillars fill out your professional story.

o Pillars are additional support statements that fill out your professional brand.

o Pillars are your credentials, your notable successes, and, done right, they can be targeted to the audience you are addressing.

o Pillars highlight achievements, provide answers to common questions or objections. They are the correct place for your industry jargon.

o Pillars are flexible; you can mix and match them based on the audience.

- In pillars, you can include:

  o Credentials

  o Company (organization) name

  o Quantitative facts

- Pillars can:

  o Be used for internal meetings/colleague introductions

  o Highlight the important aspects of your professional achievements

  o Answer common questions/objections

  o Be a place for your industry jargon

  o Be used for internal meetings

  o Dissect your elevator speech or 30-second drill and you'll probably find your pillars in there.

  o Unravelling the pillars that are likely stuck in your 30-second drill allows you the flexibility to use each one separately, one at a time, whenever they are most useful and impactful.

- Making your pillars good and brief takes time. Take time to craft every pillar you use. Pillars follow the rules of being simple, clear, authentic and (relatively) brief. The best pillars are well thought out and scripted. If they are practiced enough, they slip off the tongue and sound so natural to the listener/reader that it might be assumed the pillar was spoken for the first time, on the fly. That sound of spontaneity lends itself to authenticity. Not only does "authentic" mean *truthful*, it also means *heartfelt* and *sincere*. A great combination for your listener to hear and remember.

- When using your pillars in person or online, choose the one(s) that your audience is most likely to be interested in. Remember, people are most interested in themselves.

- Archetypes three and four (of seven):
  o *My Work in a Bigger Context*
  o *The Results of What I Do*

Chapter Five

- The Art of Hello is not:
  o An advertisement for your employer
  o Bragging
  o Everything you have ever accomplished
  o A one liner
  o Life-long and permanent
  o An asset your career can be without

Chapter Six

- The ROI on a well-crafted Art of Hello introduction is huge.

- Use your Art of Hello introduction everywhere that you want to be seen and known for your professional achievements.

- Spending only one hour to make your professional brand ready for prime time will net a huge ROI on your time.

- Your Art of Hello introduction will be:
  o A one-of-a-kind asset in your professional arsenal
  o A lead source, since others can remember and refer you
  o The agent of your advocacy circle
  o Used to introduce yourself, in a way that makes you memorable
  o A tool that differentiates you from others

- The same six to ten words are durable assets that can be used:
  o For in-person introductions
  o On Zoom and other platforms for daily meetings
  o At the top of your LinkedIn profile and in your summary
  o To introduce yourself on all your social media sites
  o In the executive summary of your resume
  o On your business card, front or back
  o In your email signature block
  o On your voicemail greeting

o In your bio and on your company website

o Anywhere you want to be seen and known for your professional achievements

Chapter Seven

- Well-crafted Art of Hello introductions have impact
- Archetypes five through seven:

  o *The Essence of Who I Am*

  o *My Repeated Successes*

  o *My Aspirations*

Recap of Archetypes

1. *The Biggest, Baddest Thing I Have Done*
   Example: Karen - *I revitalize tired brands.*

2. *My Newest Accomplishment*
   Example: Shaunna - *I help manufacturing plants become LEED certified.*

3. *My Work in a Bigger Context*
   Example: Jennifer - *I am an economic development professional. I keep North Texans in water for decades to come.*

4. *The Results of What I Do*
   Example: John - *I am a billion-dollar brand builder on the back of old-fashioned brick and mortar retail.*

5. *The Essence of Who I Am*
   Example: Mike - *I help my clients become comfortable and confident in their financial futures.*

6. *My Repeated Successes*
Example: Bill - *Introducing the right people, for the right reasons, at the right time.*

7. *My Aspirations*
Example: Christina - *By day I sell cloud technology, and by heart I advocate for organ donations.*

Chapter Eight

* Avoid the Classic ~~Errors~~ Mistakes
* Skippable Mistakes

    o Mistake #1: The List Method
       The "so what" meter flicks on, and, worse, the listener zones out. Executives expect executive summaries, not lists.

    o Mistake #2: Chronological
       A resume is not an introduction. A resume is a resume. It's there for interested parties to read, not something to be hoisted upon an innocent new acquaintance. No one can remember the details of dates, titles, and companies strung together in a long introduction. The chronological introduction cannot represent a person's brand. All it says is that the person has an employment history.

    o Mistake #3: MBA-speak
       The reason so many people are lured in by this style of introduction is to sound smart. Perhaps

the most common introduction mistake made is to introduce oneself with a string of sophisticated business terms that would be the hallmark of an MBA program. Webster's defines a 50-cent word as "an obscure word used to describe a simple idea thus making the user self-important."

Problems with MBA-speak Introductions:

- Loss of concentration by the listener
- The potential for mis-matched interpretation
- Can it be remembered? (I don't think so.)
- The potential for advocacy is lost. In order for a person to act on your behalf when you are not present, your brand must be clear as a bell. MBA-speak doesn't lean in that direction.

o Mistake #4: Your Job Title

In a LinkedIn search of the United State, the primary tool to introduce themselves by nearly ten million people was the same: Project Manager. A more thoughtful introduction would put every one of those nearly ten million people on the path to a more descriptive, useful, and memorable introduction. Think about the meaning of the title beyond the fact that it is assigned to you. Consider the brand promise of the job and start thinking about how you would like to be known.

o Mistake #5: Degree Name
A person is more and delivers more than the degree title describes. Degree titles tend to be generic, the same from college to college.

o Mistake #6: Inconsistency
Every brand-building expert will state that consistency is core to building brands.

Reinforcement is important in forming memories because it moves the memory relationship from short-lived categories to longer-lasting ones. Repetition matters in establishing your personal/professional brand.

Chapter Nine

- The Art of Hello is for job seekers and the rest of us. For anyone who who cares about their professional life and brand, The Art of Hello is an important career asset.

  o For the job seeker, The Art of Hello introduction:

    - demonstrates conscious competence
    - is a personal brand
    - is a way to quickly identify yourself
    - ensures you are ready when opportunity knocks
    - is a big arrow in your job-search quiver

- o Use your Art of Hello introduction as your Title, put your pillars in the Summary section of LinkedIn.
- The Art of Hello and its use by introverts
  - o As many as 30 to 50 percent of the population are introverts.
  - o The Art of Hello introductions and pillars are perfect tools for introverts.
  - o Knowing what to say about yourself is comfortable and can reduce the stress of being pushed into social situations.
- The Art of Hello is useful for senior executives because there is a richness to a person's career by the second decade of their work life and beyond; it is a fertile field for describing one's work in an Art of Hello introduction.
- Colloquial Sells
  - o Appropriately used, colloquial Art of Hello language is similar to the concept of classy—it is easier to recognize it than it is to describe.
  - o Colloquial language creates images or pictures with words.
  - o Some people are more casual, upbeat, and prefer less formal language.
  - o The colloquial option is perfect for a person who feels that something catchy and informal suits their brand.

Chapter Ten

Three Steps to Creating an Art of Hello Introduction of Your Own

1. Hear Yourself/Know Yourself - The first step in creating your own Art of Hello introduction is to hear yourself/know yourself. The purpose of this step is to examine your professional outcomes to identify the patterns that represent the brand promise you make in your daily work.

    *   This step, which defines your deliverables, brand promise, and successes that are the hallmark of your work, is done by storytelling.

    *   Partner up and tell stories.

    *   Be successful, be sure you allow yourself and your listener-partner to generalize the impact of your work and stories.

2. Build Your Pillars - Pillars support and fill out your professional brand. To use them well, remember that their job is to:

    *   Highlight the important aspects of your professional achievements—an advanced degree or professional credentials

    *   Focus on your points of pride. The work you have done that sets you apart and constitutes the *biggest, baddest things you have done*, or that shines a light on your best professional qualities

- Help you anticipate an objection or concern, or to get a jump on a career question that comes your way
- Provide a place for the best use of industry or professional jargon
- Should be scripted and memorized
- Are also for internal organization introductions
- Provide a place where numbers shine
- Pillars follow the simple, clear, authentic, and rather brief rules of The Art of Hello introduction. Sure, you have more than six to ten words to spend on any pillar, but you still want to craft them tightly. They'll be easier to say and easier to remember.

3. Test your Art of Hello introduction
   - Gut check - This is an important "gut test." No matter how good The Art of Hello phrase sounds, if it is not right for you, it's not right.
   - CASBAH - Your Art of Hello introduction needs to pass the test of being *Clear, Actual, Specific, Brief, Authentic* and *Honest*.
     - o The primary emphasis of the CASBAH test is authenticity and brevity.
     - o Once authenticity and brevity are confirmed, test for clarity.
     - o The ruination of clarity is most likely the attractive lure of MBA-speak.

- Phone a friend

- Call an old colleague, current colleague, past boss, or advisor. Read them your introduction and ask if they think it represents you well. Ask if they can repeat your introduction back to you.

- Repetition of your Art of Hello introduction is like hearing a song over again. Each time you hear it, it becomes more memorable.

Chapter Eleven

Delivering on the Promise of The Art of Hello: Testimonials

- Susan: *I build and fix internal communications.* Lesson: Less is more.

- Peggy: *I work with professionals and their families to help them become work optional.* Lesson: Your Art of Hello introduction can incite applause.

- Adrienne: *Communications professional with a passion for employee engagement and storytelling.* Lesson: The right introduction can get you the right attention.

- Cindy: *I simplify the hiring process.* Lesson: Nothing beats clear, simple, and brief for getting the introduction response you deserve.

- Mitra: *I love to make computers run faster.* Lesson: Technical jargon may not enrich the opportunity to distinguish yourself. Lesson: Go simple and back it up with more detailed pillars.

- McKee: *I help companies find money with projects, processes, and people.* Lesson: Increase engagement through simplicity and clarity.
- Jennifer: *Elevating the careers of ambitious women.* Lesson: Having a crystal clear and appealing Art of Hello brand statement has many benefits. Growing your valued LinkedIn network is just one of them.